# Everyone Needs a
# WILL

# Everyone Needs a
# WILL

If you don't have a will, the state
will decide who gets your property

**Martin S. Bender
Attorney at Law**

**BOB ADAMS, INC.**
PUBLISHERS
Holbrook, Massachusetts

Published by
Bob Adams, Inc.
260 Center Street
Holbrook, MA 02343

Printed in the United States of America.

ISBN: 1-55850-861-9

A  B  C  D  E  F  G  H  I  J

YOUR WILL IS AN IMPORTANT LEGAL DOCUMENT. HAVE A QUALIFIED LEGAL PROFESSIONAL REVIEW IT TO VERIFY THAT IT IS COMPLETE AND FAITHFUL TO YOUR WISHES, THAT IT WILL DIRECT YOUR PROPERTY WHERE YOU WANT IT TO GO, AND THAT IT WILL MINIMIZE THE TAXES ON YOUR ESTATE. LAWS CAN CHANGE; TELL YOUR ATTORNEY TO CONTACT YOU IF LAWS CHANGE IN SUCH A WAY AS TO MATERIALLY AFFECT YOUR WILL.

This publication contains material and information which has been gathered from sources believed to be accurate, but the author and publisher cannot guarantee the reliability of the material and information since they are based on laws which are subject to change or to differing interpretations.

The author and publisher cannot, of course, certify that the forms in this publication will be used for the purposes intended, and thus assume no responsibility for their improper use.

# Contents

**Appendix**
**Will Forms**

# Introduction

The majority of Americans die without leaving a Will, or in legal language, these people die "intestate." Their families and loved ones must then become involved with the state laws and regulations that apply when someone dies intestate. After your relative or loved one has departed without leaving a Will, his or her property will be distributed to the person or persons designated by the applicable state law, which also decides who will be named as legal guardian of his or her minor children and of the minor children's property. In effect, the state decides who gets the property and who controls the destiny of the minor children of your relative or loved one. The deceased's intentions are disregarded by the court, since they are not known, and it is very likely that the decisions of the court will differ substantially from the intentions of the deceased. The only way that the deceased can legally make his or her intentions known after death, is by writing a legally valid Will.

What problems or risks do people tend to encounter in writing Wills? There are three main stumbling blocks: leaving people out, failing to revise the Will when there are major fluctuations in property value, and neglecting to have an attorney review the Will at the outset and whenever there are changes made to it.

It is only by having a legally valid Will, that you, your family, and loved ones will have the security of knowing that the ultimate decisions regarding your home, your bank accounts, your car, and your children will be made by you and not by the state.

*Everyone Needs a Will* gives you the opportunity to write your own Will. Residents of every state except Louisiana may use this book to write a legal Will. After completing your Will, have a qualified legal professional review it to verify that it is complete and faithful to your wishes, that it will direct your property where you want it to go, and that it will minimize the taxes on your estate. Laws can change; tell your attorney to contact you if laws change in such a way as to materially affect your will.

## How This Book Is Organized

This book is organized in the following way. There are 10 model Wills which also include a model Affidavit of Subscribing Witnesses. These models cover situations where you, the person who is preparing the Will, is either married or unmarried at the time of preparation of your Will, and further, which one of the following four categories you fall into:

a)  have minor children but no adult children

b)  have minor children and adult children

c)  have adult children but no minor children

d)  have no children

The first eight model Wills that follow are classified according to your marital status and category regarding children. Model Wills 9 and 10, show you how to make specific bequests, which will be discussed later. The best way to understand what a Will is all about is to look at a model Will, which has been prepared for a fictitious person to serve as an example for you as to how you may prepare your Will.

Following the model Wills 2 through 10, in the Appendix, you will find the blank Will forms, instructions and accompanying Affidavit of Subscribing Witnesses forms. You will later use the appropriate blank Will form to make your Will.

Before we look at model Will number 1, let us discuss the legal terms for the persons referred to in the Will.

### Testator and Testatrix

The most important person is the Testator or Testatrix (Testator is male, Testatrix is female). The Testator or Testatrix is the person of legal age who prepares or writes the Will, and signs and dates the Will.

### Executor and Executrix

The Executor or Executrix (Executor is male, Executrix is female) is the person that you name in the Will to carry out the terms of your Will and to administer the estate (estate is all of the property that a person owns).

### Beneficiary

The Beneficiary (or Beneficiaries) is the person, persons, or organizations to whom you decide to leave all, or part, of your estate.

### Witnesses

The Witnesses are the people who after seeing the Testator (or Testatrix) sign and date the Will and declare that this is his/her Will, witness the Will by signing their names and listing their home addresses at the end of the Will.

### Guardian and Co-guardian

The Guardian or Co-guardians (if you have minor children) are the person or persons whom you choose to be legally responsible for the care of your minor children and their property. Of course, you should check in advance with both guardians and Executors and obtain their agreement with regard to the roles they will be taking on. It is recommended that you arrange for auxiliary or "backup" Executors and guardians; discuss this with your attorney.

Now that you have an understanding of the legal terms that are a basic part of a Will, let us look at model Will number 1, which is the Last Will and Testament of Mary G. Smith, a married woman with minor children. Mary G. Smith is a fictitious person and is used for example purposes only. The model has a front side, a back side, and an optional Affidavit of Subscribing Witnesses. Each of these three (3) pages has an explanation page following that page. Please note that the Affidavit of Subscribing Witnesses is optional and is not needed in order to make the Will a legal Will. Please read Model Will number 1 and the accompanying explanation pages carefully.

Your Will is an important legal document. Have a qualified legal professional review it to verify that it is complete and faithful to your wishes, that it will direct your property where you want it to go, and that it will minimize the taxes on your estate. Laws can change; tell your attorney to contact you if laws change in such a way as to materially affect your will.

# Last Will and Testament
# of

_Mary G. Smith_

I, _Mary G. Smith_, presently residing at
_5 Bay Drive, Queens, New York_,
being of full age and sound and disposing mind and memory, hereby make, publish and declare this to be my Last Will and Testament.

FIRST: I hereby revoke any and all Wills and Codicils by me anytime heretofore made.

SECOND: I direct all of my just debts and funeral expenses be paid out of my Estate as soon as practicable after my death.

THIRD: I am presently married to _David R. Smith_.

FOURTH: I hereby give, devise and bequeath all of my Estate, real, personal and mixed, of every kind and nature whatsoever and wheresoever situated, to my beloved husband absolutely and forever.

FIFTH: In the event that my husband shall predecease me, then and in that event, I give, devise and bequeath my Estate hereinabove mentioned in paragraph "FOURTH" herein, to my beloved child or children or grandchildren surviving me, per stirpes.

SIXTH: In the event I am not survived by my husband or any children, or grandchildren, then, and in such event, I give, devise and bequeath my said Estate to the following named beneficiary/beneficiaries or their survivor/survivors in equal shares.

a. _Edward Jones, 123 East 23rd Street, NY, NY_
Name and address of beneficiary

b. _American Cancer Society, New York Chapter_
Name and address of beneficiary

c. _____
Name and address of beneficiary

d. _____
Name and address of beneficiary

e. _____
Name and address of beneficiary

# Glossary

The numbers on this page correspond to the numbers on the model will on the previous page. Important words are defined, and important aspects of the model will are explained.

1. A Last Will & Testament, known simply as a "WILL," is a written declaration of how a person intends his property to be disposed of after his death.

2. The Testatrix is Mary G. Smith, the person who is writing the will, and who signs and dates the will.

3. A will must have the full name of the Testatrix. It is important that the spelling and middle initial, if any, are accurate.

4. A will should also have the Testatrix's address.

5. The Testatrix must have the mental capacity to make a will.

6. The will revokes or cancels all former wills and codicils. A codicil is used to add to, remove from, or modify the provisions of a will, and must be signed, declared, and witnessed in the same way as a will.

7. Mary is including a provision to pay all of her outstanding bills and funeral expenses.

8. David is Mary's husband.

9. ESTATE—An estate is all of the property that a person owns.

10. GIVE, DEVISE, and BEQUEATH—This is the act of giving away your real estate and personal property by will. "Devise" relates to real estate and "bequeath" relates to personal property.

11. Mary leaves everything to her husband David.

12. Predecease—to die before. If a husband predeceases a wife, then he has passed away before her.

13. If David passes away before Mary, Mary leaves everything to her children.

14. PER STIRPES—An example of a per stirpes distribution is the following: If Mary G. Smith has 3 children (Beth, Karen, and Susan) and leaves her estate to her 3 children in equal amounts, then under a per stirpes distribution, if Beth passed away before her mother (and left two children), then the 1/3 share that Beth would have been entitled to is passed on to her children so that they each get 1/2 of their mother's share.

15. The Beneficiary is the person, persons, and/or organizations to whom you decide to leave all, or part, of your estate.

16. If David and Mary's children and grandchildren pass away before Mary, then Mary leaves everything to her brother Edward Jones.

17      SEVENTH: I hereby nominate and appoint my beloved husband to be the Executor of this, my Last Will and Testament, and I direct that no bond or other security shall be required of him in any jurisdiction. If my said husband is unable to serve as Executor, then I nominate and appoint ___Edward Jones_____ ,

18      Executor/Executrix of this my Last Will and Testament, and I further direct that he/she not be required to post any bond or other security.

19      EIGHTH: I hereby nominate and appoint my husband as Guardian of the

20 person and property of my minor children. In the event that my husband shall be unable to serve as Guardian, then, and in such event I nominate and appoint

21 ___Edward Jones and his wife Kay Jones_____ ,
Guardian/Co-guardians of the person and property of my minor child or children, and I direct that no bond shall be required of any Guardian herein.

     NINTH: I give to my Executor/Executrix, authority to exercise all the powers, duties, rights

22 and immunities conferred upon fiduciaries by law with full power to sell to mortgage and to lease, and to invest and reinvest all or any part of my Estate on such terms as he/she deems best.

23      IN WITNESS WHEREOF, I hereunto set my hand this ___11___ day of ___march___, 19_89_.

                            ___mary G. Smith___
                                      (SIGN HERE)

     Signed, sealed, published and declared by the above named Testatrix, as and for her Last Will and Testament, in the presence of us, who at her request, in her presence, and in the presence of one another have hereunto subscribed our names as attesting witnesses, the day and year last written above.

24 ___Jack White___ residing at ___123 Rose Street___
                                    ___Queens, New York___

___Tina White___ residing at ___123 Rose Street___
                                    ___Queens, New York___

___Fran White___ residing at ___123 Rose Street___
                                    ___Queens, New York___

# Glossary

The numbers on this page correspond to the numbers on the model will on the previous page. Important words are defined, and important aspects of the model will are explained.

17. The Executor/Executrix is the person that you name in the will to carry out the terms of your will and to administer the estate. The person writing the will (Testatrix) often will name the beneficiary of the largest portion of the estate as Executor/Executrix. However, the Executor/Executrix is not legally required to be a beneficiary. Your will form provides that the Executor/Executrix not be required to post a bond for the Court.

18. Mary appoints her husband to settle the affairs of her estate. If David is unavailable Mary appoints her brother Edward Jones.

19. The Guardian/Co-guardians—the person whom you choose to be legally responsible for the care of your minor children and their property.

20. The Minor child/children—children who are not yet of legal age.

21. Mary appoints David to be the guardian of their minor children. If David is unavailable Mary appoints her brother and sister-in-law.

22. Mary gives David total discretion subject to state law to carry out the terms of the will.

23. Mary dates and signs the will in front of the witnesses.

24. The Witnesses are the people who after seeing the Testatrix sign and date the will and declare that this is her will, witness the will by signing their names and listing their home addresses at the end of the will. The witnesses must be together and see you sign the will. Most states require only 2 witnesses, but some states require 3 witnesses. Your will form includes 3 signature lines for your protection. The witnesses should be of sound mind, and not be named as beneficiaries in the will.

Affidavit of Subscribing Witnesses

STATE OF __New York__ )

                     ss.:

COUNTY OF __Queens__ )

     On __march 11__, 19__89__, personally appeared before me, the undersigned authority

1. __mary G. Smith__         2. __Jack White__
       Testatrix                         Witness

3. __Tina White__          4. __Fran White__
       Witness                         Witness

known to me to be the Testatrix and Witnesses, respectively, who being severally sworn state under oath that, all the subscribing witnesses witnessed the execution of the Will of the within named Testatrix on the same date they subscribed this instrument; the Testatrix in their presence, subscribed the Will at the end and at the time of making the subscription declared the instrument to be the Testatrix's Last Will and Testament; at the request of the Testatrix and in the Testatrix's sight and presence and in the sight and presence of each other, all the subscribing witnesses witnessed the execution of the Will by the Testatrix by subscribing their names as witnesses to it; the Testatrix at the time of the execution of the Will, was over the age of 18 years and appeared to them of sound mind, memory and understanding and was in all respects competent to make a Will; and the Testatrix having declared to the said witnesses that she was not under any duress or any undue influence and that she voluntarily executed this will as her free act and deed.

     The subscribing witnesses further state that this affidavit was executed at the request of the Testatrix, and at the time of the execution of this affidavit the original Will, above described, was exhibited to them and they identified it as such Will by their signatures appearing on it as subscribing witnesses.

     The Testatrix states that each witness was and is competent and of a proper age to witness a will and further acknowledges that she has read the within instrument and she affirms that each and every statement made by the subscribing witness is true to her own knowledge.

Severally subscribed,            TESTATRIX: __Mary G. Smith__
acknowledged and sworn to
before me on __march 11, 1989__    WITNESS: __Jack White__
__Tom Dolan__
Notary Public or Person          WITNESS: __Tina White__
Authorized to Take Oaths

                              WITNESS: __Fran White__

# Instructions for Completing the Affidavit of Subscribing Witnesses

An Affidavit of Subscribing Witnesses (also known as a self-proving affidavit) which is recognized in most states is also included in the will kit. This Affidavit allows you to self-prove your will. A will does not require this affidavit in order for the will to be valid. However, this affidavit may save much time and expense when a will is being probated. A situation in which this might occur is if the witnesses to the will could not be located when the will was being probated. By the will being self-proved, the witnesses will most likely not have to appear in court. A will is self-proved when the Testator (the person who writes the will) and the witnesses to the will, declare that this document is the Testator's will, and that it was properly executed, and sign this affidavit before an officer authorized to administer oaths or a notary public. This affidavit is included in the will and should be used if possible, but again, a will is valid without an affidavit of subscribing witnesses.

If you choose to self-prove your will, use the following instructions:

1. You must sign your will and have it witnessed by three witnesses, and follow the instructions for the execution of a will, as they are given in this book.

2. If there is not an officer authorized to administer oaths or a notary public present at the will signing, you and the witnesses to the will must at a later time, personally appear before such officer or a notary public. All parties must bring proper identification. Advise the officer or notary public that you want to self-prove your will. Ask the officer or notary public if he or she has a form for this purpose. If yes, follow the officer or notary's instructions.

3. If the officer or notary does not have a form, use the Affidavit of Subscribing Witnesses included in this kit.

4. Use the model affidavit of subscribing witnesses as a guide to filling out your affidavit. You and your witnesses should write your names in the spaces designated "Testator" and "witness." The officer or notary will have you swear to the statements made in the affidavit, and to sign your names at the bottom of the affidavit. The officer or notary will date, sign, and place a stamp or seal on the affidavit.

5. At this time, staple the affidavit to the will so that it becomes the last page.

# General Information

## Who may write a Will?

Any person who is 18 years of age or older may make a Will. Under certain limited circumstances in some states, a person may make a Will if they are under the age of 18. Examples of such a circumstance may be someone who is married or serving in the armed forces of the United States of America. If you are under 18, do not make a Will until after you have consulted with a lawyer.

## Selecting witnesses for your will

It is not necessary that you reveal the contents of your Will to the witnesses. The witnesses are people of legal age who after seeing you sign and date your Will and declare that this is your Will, witness the Will by signing their names and listing their home addresses at the end of the Will. The witnesses must all be present when you sign the Will. Most states require only two (2) witnesses, but some states require three (3) witnesses. All 10 of the Will forms include 3 signature lines and it is suggested you use three (3) witnesses for your protection. The witnesses should be of sound mind and may not be named as beneficiaries in the Will.

## Selecting an Executor or Executrix for your Will

The most important reason for selecting an Executor or Executrix is that you trust that person completely. That person is usually a friend or relative and may be a beneficiary. Since you have complete trust in this person, it is not necessary for them to post a bond to insure that they fulfill their duties. This also avoids expense to the Estate. For this reason all 10 will forms do not require the Executor or Executrix to post a bond.

## Selecting a guardian for your minor child (children) and their property

Generally speaking, if one parent dies, the other parent under normal circumstances would legally have the right to guardianship of the minor child (children). However, where both parents die simultaneously, or one dies and the other declines guardianship or is legally incapable of being appointed guardian, or one is already dead and the other now dies, you should name a guardian to cover such situations. It is with the greatest of thought that you must contemplate whom you would want to take care of your children and their property. After you have made a decision, you must ascertain that the person or couple that you desire to become guardian or co-guardians, are ready, willing, and able to undertake the responsibility for your child (children) and their property.

## If I am married, what property can I give by will?

A married couple's property ownership situation is usually more complicated than a single person's. In community property states, namely Arizona, California, Idaho, Nevada, New Mexico, Texas, Washington, and Wisconsin, spouses usually share property ownership even though one spouse's name is on the title or deed. In most common law property states, (namely, all states other than these listed in this paragraph, with the exception of Louisiana) a spouse is entitled to one third of the property left in the Will. In a few states, it is one-half.

If you use Will forms 1, 2, 3, or 4, then you need not be concerned with the information contained in this paragraph because these Will forms leave the entire estate to your surviving spouse. Likewise, if you use Will forms 9 and 10 and you leave at least 50% of your estate to your surviving spouse, you need not be further concerned. However, if you use Will forms 9 or 10, and it is your intention to leave less than 50% of your estate to your surviving spouse, then it is your responsibility to check the laws of the state of your residence or consult a local attorney, because if you leave your spouse less than the legal minimum, he or she may elect to "take against the Will," and you may cause your estate a legal problem.

### What happens if I get divorced?

If you get divorced, your Will is automatically revoked as to your former spouse in many states, but not in all states. Worse, in several states, divorce revokes the entire Will. Therefore, it is strongly urged, regardless of the state you live in, if you get divorced make a new Will.

### Do I have to leave equal amounts of my estate to my children?

No. While most parents choose to leave equal amounts of their estate to their children, this does not have to be the case. You can leave unequal amounts to your children, and you may use Will forms 9 or 10 for this purpose.

### Can I disinherit my children or grandchildren?

In most states you can disinherit anyone you choose other than your spouse. If you wish to disinherit a child you should state this in your Will (for example, "I disinherit my son Peter, for I do not want him to receive anything from my es-

tate"). Will forms 9 or 10 could be used for this purpose.

If you wish to disinherit a grandchild whose parent (your child) is dead, you should specifically disinherit the grandchild. Again, Will forms 9 or 10 could be used for this purpose.

If you wish to disinherit a grandchild whose parent (your child) is alive, it is not necessary to specifically disinherit the grandchild in the Will.

### Federal estate tax considerations

Federal estate taxes are due when an estate is greater than $600,000.00. However, you are allowed to leave an unlimited amount of property to your spouse without incurring federal estate tax liability. (Of course, when the second spouse dies, this tax advantage is no longer in effect.) If your estate is substantial or complex, it is recommended that you consult a competent professional person for financial and tax planning.

### Other tax considerations

Each state varies as far as state estate taxes and inheritance taxes are concerned. Some states do not have any state estate taxes or inheritance taxes. If you have any questions regarding your state, contact the Department of Taxation in your state.

### Selecting the Will form for your situation

Now that you are more familiar with Will terms and how a Will form appears when filled out, the next step is to choose the Will form that is appropriate for your needs. There are 10 model Wills and accompanying model Affidavits of Subscribing Witnesses. You have seen the first model Will. Model Wills 2–10 appear on the following pages. After that are the blank Will forms, instructions, and accompanying Affidavit of Subscribing Witnesses forms. You will later use the appropriate blank Will form to make your Will.

Use the following chart to determine which Will form is appropriate for your situation.

**Married Woman**
**with Minor Children**
#1 Will
#9 Will

**Married Man**
**with Minor Children**
#2 Will
#9 Will

**Unmarried Individual**
**with Minor Children**
#5 Will
#9 Will

**Married Woman**
**without Minor Children**
#3 Will
#10 Will

**Married Man**
**without Minor Children**
#4 Will
#10 Will

**Unmarried Individual**
**without Minor Children**
#6 Will
#7 Will
#8 Will
#10 Will

**Guidelines for Wills #1 through #10.**

Wills #1, #2, #3, and #4 provide that a married man or married woman will leave all of their estate to their husband or wife, and that if their husband or wife does not survive them, then everything is left to their children equally. Will #9 which is for a married man, married woman, or unmarried person, who have minor children, has paragraph "SIXTH" which provides for you to leave specific gifts (bequests) to anyone (i.e., church, friends, etc.) and to divide up your estate as you see fit.

Will #10 is the same as Will #9 except that Will #10 is for a married man, married woman, or unmarried person without minor children, while Will #9 is for those same people with minor children.

Will #5 provides that an unmarried person leaves everything to their children in equal shares.

Use Will #5 if you have both minor children and adult children.

Will #6 provides that an unmarried person leaves everything to their adult children in equal shares.

Will #7 provides for an unmarried person with no children to leave their entire estate to one person (beneficiary) and in the event that person is not alive, then the estate is left to another person.

Will #8 provides for an unmarried person with no children to leave their estate to two or more persons (beneficiaries) equally. If two beneficiaries are named, they will each get 50% of the estate, if three are named they will each get 33% of the estate, etc....

To summarize, #1 Will is to be used by a married woman with minor children.

#2 Will is to be used by a married man with minor children.

The #1 and #2 Wills would be used by a married couple with minor children.

#3 Will is to be used by a married woman without minor children.

The #4 Will is to be used by a married man without minor children.

The #3 and #4 Wills would be used by a married couple without minor children.

#5 Will is to be used by an unmarried person with minor children, or an unmarried person with minor children and adult children.

#6 Will is to be used by an unmarried person with adult children.

#7 Will is to used by an unmarried person with no children and one beneficiary.

#8 Will is to be used by an unmarried person with no children and two or more beneficiaries.

#9 Will is to be used by a married woman, married man, or unmarried person with minor children making specific bequests.

A "specific bequest" is the giving of an identifiable thing which is part of the Testator's estate or a stated sum of money to a specific person. Examples, are as follows:

*"I give, devise, and bequeath my 1988 FORD ESCORT to my nephew, Jeff Jones,"* or

*"I give, devise, and bequeath my gold diamond necklace to my friend, Sally Smith,"* or

*"I give, devise, and bequeath $500.00 to my nephew, Albert Green."*

#10 Will is to be used by a married woman, married man, or unmarried person without minor children making specific bequests.

Use #9 Will only if you have minor children (or minor children and adult children).

Now is the time to fill out the Will form which is most appropriate for your situation. If you are having any difficulties with any of the materials,

please do not hesitate to seek additional assistance. By using *Everyone Needs a Will* to organize your thoughts and wishes you will save time and expense when you verify your Will with a lawyer or other professional. Select the Will which applies to your particular situation and turn to that number model Will. Read the model Will. Then remove or photocpy onto a single sheet of paper that number Will form from the back of these materials, along with the instructions for that Will form, and if you choose, the affidavit of subscribing witnesses form and the instructions for the affidavit (which are shown after the model Wills).

Place the model Will so that you can look at the model Will, the Will form, and the instructions for that Will form at the same time. Complete the Will form, and then call in your witnesses and sign the Will in the presence of the witnesses, carefully following the above instructions. Then, have a qualified legal professional review the Will to verify that it is complete and faithful to your wishes.

## I've completed my Will—storage and safekeeping

Congratulations! You have completed your Will. It goes without saying that a Will be kept in a safe place. The Executor or Executrix should know exactly where the Will is located. Your home or office are among the best places to store your Will. Safe deposit boxes can cause problems, after a death, since under the laws of certain states, the safe deposit box is sealed by government authorities. That is why your home or office is the preferred location to store your will.

## Under what circumstances should I update my Will?

1. The Executor of Executrix or alternate dies.

2. The guardian or co-guardian or alternate dies.

3. A beneficiary or alternate-beneficiary dies.

4. You get married.

5. You get divorced.

6. You have a new child or a living child dies.

7. You change your mind as to beneficiaries or bequests.

8. Major change in the value of your estate (if it affects the intent of your Will; for example, you bequeath a car to your friend, and the car is stolen and never returned, or, if you win the lottery and now require estate planning).

# Last Will and Testament
# of

2 _____David R. Smith_____

3  I, __David R. Smith_____, presently residing at

4  __5 Bay Drive, Queens, New York_____,

5  being of full age and sound and disposing mind and memory, hereby make, publish and declare this to be my Last Will and Testament.

6  FIRST: I hereby revoke any and all Wills and Codicils by me anytime heretofore made.

7  SECOND: I direct all of my just debts and funeral expenses be paid out of my Estate as soon as practicable after my death.

8  THIRD: I am presently married to __Mary G. Smith_____.

9  FOURTH: I hereby give, devise and bequeath all of my Estate, real, personal

10  and mixed, of every kind and nature whatsoever and wheresoever situated, to my

11  beloved wife absolutely and forever.

12  FIFTH: In the event that my wife shall predecease me, then and in that

13  event, I give, devise and bequeath my Estate hereinabove mentioned in paragraph "FOURTH"

14  herein, to my beloved child or children or grandchildren surviving me, per stirpes.

SIXTH: In the event I am not survived by my wife or any children, or grandchildren, then, and in such event, I give, devise and bequeath my said Estate to the following named

15  beneficiary/beneficiaries or their survivor/survivors in equal shares.

16  a. __Edward Jones, 123 East 23rd Street, NY, NY__
Name and address of beneficiary

b. _____
Name and address of beneficiary

c. _____
Name and address of beneficiary

d. _____
Name and address of beneficiary

e. _____
Name and address of beneficiary

# Glossary

The numbers on this page correspond to the numbers on the model will on the previous page. Important words are defined, and important aspects of the model will are explained.

1. A Last Will & Testament, known simply as a "Will," is a written declaration of how a person intends his property to be disposed of after his death.

2. The Testator is David R. Smith, the person who is writing the will, and who signs and dates the will.

3. A will must have the full name of the Testator. It is important that the spelling and middle initial, if any, are accurate.

4. A will should also have the Testator's address.

5. The Testator must have the mental capacity to make a will.

6. The will revokes or cancels all former wills and codicils. A codicil is used to add to, remove from, or modify the provisions of a will, and must be signed, declared, and witnessed in the same way as a will.

7. David is including a provision to pay all of his outstanding bills and funeral expenses.

8. Mary is David's wife.

9. ESTATE — An estate is all of the property that a person owns.

10. GIVE, DEVISE, and BEQUEATH — This is the act of giving away your real estate and personal property by will. "Devise" relates to real estate and "bequeath" relates to personal property.

11. David leaves everything to his wife, Mary.

12. Predecease — to die before. If a wife predeceases a husband, then she has passed away before him.

13. If Mary passes away before David, David leaves everything to his children.

14. PER STIRPES — An example of a per stirpes distribution is the following: If David R. Smith has 3 children (Beth, Karen, and Susan) and leaves his estate to his 3 children in equal amounts, then under a per stirpes distribution, if Beth passed away before her father (and left two children), then the 1/3 share that Beth would have been entitled to is passed on to her children so that they each get 1/2 of their mother's share.

15. The Beneficiary is the person, persons, and/or organizations to whom you decide to leave all, or part of your estate.

16. If David and Mary's children and grandchildren pass away before David, then David leaves everything to his brother-in-law Edward Jones. David did not have to name a relative. David could have named a friend, friends, other relatives, or organizations such as a church. Each beneficiary named in paragraph 6 would take equally with the other beneficiary or beneficiaries. For example, if David named 2 friends and the First Presbyterian Church, then each beneficiary would receive 1/3 of David's estate.

17    SEVENTH: I hereby nominate and appoint my beloved wife to be the Executrix of this, my Last Will and Testament, and I direct that no bond or other security shall be required of her
18    in any jurisdiction. If my said wife is unable to serve as Executrix, then I nominate and appoint _Edward Jones_, Executor/Executrix of this my Last Will and Testament, and I further direct that he/she not be required to post any bond or other security.

19    EIGHTH: I hereby nominate and appoint my wife as Guardian of the person and
20    property of my minor children. In the event that my wife shall be unable to serve as Guardian,
21    then, and in such event I nominate and appoint _Edward Jones + his wife Kay Jones_, Guardian/-Co-guardians of the person and property of my minor child or children, and I direct that no bond shall be required of any Guardian herein.

NINTH: I give to my Executor/Executrix, authority to exercise all the powers, duties,
22    rights, and immunities conferred upon fiduciaries by law with full power to sell to mortgage and to lease, and to invest and reinvest all or any part of my Estate on such terms as he/she deems best.

23    IN WITNESS WHEREOF, I hereunto set my hand this ____11____ day of __march__, 19_89_.

_David R. Smith_
(SIGN HERE)

Signed, sealed, published and declared by the above named Testator, as and for his Last Will and Testament, in the presence of us, who at his request, in his presence, and in the presence of one another have hereunto subscribed our names as attesting witnesses, the day and year last written above.

24    _Jack White_        residing at    _123 Rose Street_
                                        _Queens, New York_

      _Tina White_        residing at    _123 Rose Street_
                                        _Queens, New York_

      _Fran White_        residing at    _123 Rose Street_
                                        _Queens, New York_

# Glossary

The numbers on this page correspond to the numbers on the model will on the previous page. Important words are defined, and important aspects of the model will are explained.

17. The Executor/Executrix is the person that you name in the will to carry out the terms of your will and to administer the estate. The person writing the will (Testator) often will name the beneficiary of the largest portion of the estate as Executor/Executrix. However, the Executor/Executrix is not legally required to be a beneficiary. Your will form provides that the Executor/Executrix not be required to post a bond for the Court.

18. David appoints his wife to settle the affairs of his estate. If Mary is unavailable, David appoints his brother-in-law Edward Jones.

19. The Guardian/Co-guardians — the person whom you choose to be legally responsible for the care of your minor children and their property.

20. The Minor child/children — children who are not yet of legal age.

21. David appoints Mary to be the guardian of their minor children. If Mary is unavailable, David appoints her brother and sister-in-law.

22. David gives Mary total discretion subject to state law to carry out the terms of the will.

23. David dates and signs the will in front of the witnesses.

24. The Witnesses are the people who after seeing the Testator sign and date the will and declare that this is his will, witness the will by signing their names and listing their home addresses at the end of the will. The witnesses must be together and must see you sign the will. Most states require only 2 witnesses, but some states require 3 witnesses. Your will form includes 3 signature lines for your protection. The witnesses should be of sound mind, and not be named as beneficiaries in the will.

Affidavit of Subscribing Witnesses

STATE OF _____New York_____ )
                                        ss.:
COUNTY OF _____Queens_____ )

On _____March 11_____, 19_89_, personally appeared before me, the undersigned authority

1. _____David R. Smith_____        2. _____Jack White_____
              Testator                                  Witness

3. _____Tina White_____        4. _____Fran White_____
              Witness                                   Witness

known to me to be the Testator and Witnesses, respectively, who being severally sworn state under oath
that, all the subscribing witnesses witnessed the execution of the Will of the within named Testator on the
same date they subscribed this instrument; the Testator in their presence, subscribed the Will at the end
and at the time of making the subscription declared the instrument to be the Testator's Last Will and
Testament; at the request of the Testator and in the Testator's sight and presence and in the sight and
presence of each other, all the subscribing witnesses witnessed the execution of the Will by the Testator by
subscribing their names as witnesses to it; the Testator at the time of the execution of the Will, was over
the age of 18 years and appeared to them of sound mind, memory and understanding and was in all
respects competent to make a Will; and the Testator having declared to the said witnesses that he was not
under any duress or any undue influence and that he voluntarily executed this will as his free act and deed.

The subscribing witnesses further state that this affidavit was executed at the request
of the Testator, and at the time of the execution of this affidavit the original Will, above described, was
exhibited to them and they identified it as such Will by their signatures appearing on it as subscribing
witnesses.

The Testator states that each witness was and is competent and of a proper age to witness
a will and further acknowledges that he has read the within instrument and he affirms that each and every
statement made by the subscribing witness is true to his own knowledge.

Severally subscribed,                    TESTATOR: _David R. Smith____
acknowledged and sworn to
before me on march 11, 1989              WITNESS: ___Jack White_____

_____Mark Davis_____                WITNESS: ___Tina White_____
Notary Public or Person
Authorized to Take Oaths                 WITNESS: ___Fran White_____

# Instructions for Completing the Affidavit of Subscribing Witnesses

An Affidavit of Subscribing Witnesses (also known as a self-proving affidavit) which is recognized in most states is also included in the will kit. This Affidavit allows you to self-prove your will. A will does not require this affidavit in order for the will to be valid. However, this affidavit may save much time and expense when a will is being probated. A situation in which this might occur is if the witnesses to the will could not be located when the will was being probated. By the will being self-proved, the witnesses will most likely not have to appear in court. A will is self-proved when the Testator (the person who writes the will) and the witnesses to the will, declare that this document is the Testator's will, and that it was properly executed, and sign this affidavit before an officer authorized to administer oaths or a notary public. This affidavit is included in the will and should be used if possible, but again, a will is valid without an affidavit of subscribing witnesses.

If you choose to self-prove your will, use the following instructions:

1. You must sign your will and have it witnessed by three witnesses, and follow the instructions for the execution of a will, as they are given in this book.

2. If there is not an officer authorized to administer oaths or a notary public present at the will signing, you and the witnesses to the will must at a later time personally appear before such officer or a notary public. All parties must bring proper identification. Advise the officer or notary public that you want to self-prove your will. Ask the officer or notary public if he or she has a form for this purpose. If yes, follow the officer or notary's instructions.

3. If the officer or notary does not have a form, use the Affidavit of Subscribing Witnesses included in this kit.

4. Use the model affidavit of subscribing witnesses as a guide to filling out your affidavit. You and your witnesses should write your names in the spaces designated "Testator" and "witness." The officer or notary will have you swear to the statements made in the affidavit, and to sign your names at the bottom of the affidavit. The officer or notary will date, sign, and place a stamp or seal on the affidavit.

5. At this time, staple the affidavit to the will so that it becomes the last page.

# Last Will and Testament
# of

2       _____Sally B. Hill_____

3   **I,**_____Sally B. Hill_____, presently residing at

4      ___1 Main Street, Chicago, Illinois_____,

5 being of full age and sound and disposing mind and memory, hereby make, publish and declare this to be my Last Will and Testament.

6        FIRST: I hereby revoke any and all Wills and Codicils by me anytime heretofore made.

7        SECOND: I direct all of my just debts and funeral expenses be paid out of my Estate as soon as practicable after my death.

8        THIRD: I am presently married to _____Frank S. Hill_____.

9        FOURTH: I hereby give, devise and bequeath all of my Estate, real, personal

10 and mixed, of every kind and nature whatsoever and wheresoever situated, to my

11 beloved husband absolutely and forever.

12        FIFTH: In the event that my husband shall predecease me, then and in that

13 event, I give, devise and bequeath my Estate hereinabove mentioned in paragraph "FOURTH"

14 herein, to my beloved child or children or grandchildren surviving me, per stirpes.

       SIXTH: In the event I am not survived by my husband or any children, or grandchildren, then, and in such event, I give, devise and bequeath my said Estate to the following named

15 beneficiary/beneficiaries or their survivor/survivors in equal shares.

16    a. __Alien Singer, 20 Main Street, Chicago, IL_____
Name and address of beneficiary

     b. __American Cancer Society, Chicago Chapter_____
Name and address of beneficiary

     c. _____
Name and address of beneficiary

     d. _____
Name and address of beneficiary

     e. _____
Name and address of beneficiary

# Glossary

The numbers on this page correspond to the numbers on the model will on the previous page. Important words are defined, and important aspects of the model will are explained.

1. A Last Will & Testament, known simply as a "WILL," is a written declaration of how a person intends his property to be disposed of after his death.

2. The Testatrix is Sally B. Hill, the person who is writing the will, and who signs and dates the will.

3. A will must have the full name of the Testatrix. It is important that the spelling and middle initial, if any, are accurate.

4. A will should also have the Testatrix's address.

5. The Testatrix must have the mental capacity to make a will.

6. The will revokes or cancels all former wills and codicils. A codicil is used to add to, remove from or modify the provisions of a will, and must be signed, declared and witnessed in the same way as a will.

7. Sally is including a provision to pay all of her outstanding bills and funeral expenses.

8. Frank is Sally's husband.

9. ESTATE — An estate is all of the property that a person owns.

10. GIVE, DEVISE, and BEQUEATH — This is the act of giving away your real estate and personal property by will. "Devise" relates to real estate and "bequeath" relates to personal property.

11. Sally leaves everything to her husband Frank.

12. Predecease — to die before. If a husband predeceases a wife, then he has passed away before her.

13. If Frank passes away before Sally, Sally leaves everything to her children.

14. PER STIRPES — An example of a per stirpes distribution is the following: If Sally B. Hill has 3 children (Beth, Karen, and Susan) and leaves her estate to her 3 children in equal amounts, then under a per stirpes distribution, if Beth passed away before her mother (and left two children), then the 1/3 share that Beth would have been entitled to is passed on to her children so that they each get 1/2 of their mother's share.

15. The Beneficiary is the person, persons, and/or organizations to whom you decide to leave all, or part of your estate.

16. If Frank and Sally's children and grandchildren pass away before Sally, then Sally leaves everything to her brother Allen Singer and the American Cancer Society in equal shares.

17.       SEVENTH: I hereby nominate and appoint my beloved husband to be the Executrix of this, my Last Will and Testament, and I direct that no bond or other security shall be required of him in any jurisdiction. If my said husband is unable to serve as Executor, then I nominate and

18. appoint _Allen Singer_, Executor/Executrix of this my Last Will and Testament, and I further direct that he/she not be required to post any bond or other security.

19.       EIGHTH: I give to my Executor/Executrix, authority to exercise all the powers, duties, rights and immunities conferred upon fiduciaries by law with full power to sell to mortgage and to lease, and to invest and reinvest all or any part of my Estate on such terms as he/she deems best.

20.       IN WITNESS WHEREOF, I hereunto set my hand this _____11_____ day of _march_, 19_89_.

_Sally B Hill_
(SIGN HERE)

Signed, sealed, published and declared by the above named Testatrix, as and for her Last Will and Testament, in the presence of us, who at her request, in her presence, and in the presence of one another have hereunto subscribed our names as attesting witnesses, the day and year last written above.

21. _Mark Collins_      residing at      _420 Lincoln Ave._
                                                     _Chicago, IL_

_Linda Collins_      residing at      _420 Lincoln Ave._
                                                     _Chicago, IL_

_Ralph Collins_      residing at      _420 Lincoln Ave._
                                                     _Chicago, IL_

# Glossary

The numbers on this page correspond to the numbers on the model will on the previous page. Important words are defined, and important aspects of the model will are explained.

17. The Executor/Executrix is the person that you name in the will to carry out the terms of your will and to administer the estate. The person writing the will (Testatrix) often will name the beneficiary of the largest portion of the estate as Executor/Executrix. However, the Executor/Executrix is not legally required to be a beneficiary. Your will form provides that the Executor/Executrix not be required to post a bond for the Court.

18. Sally appoints her husband to settle the affairs of her estate. If Frank is unavailable Sally appoints her brother Allen Singer.

19. Sally gives Frank total discretion subject to state law to carry out the terms of the will.

20. Sally dates and signs the will in front of the witnesses.

21. The Witnesses are the people who after seeing the Testatrix sign and date the will and declare that this is her will, witness the will by signing their names and listing their home addresses at the end of the will. The witnesses must be together and see you sign the will. Most states require only 2 witnesses, but some states require 3 witnesses. Your will form includes 3 signature lines for your protection. The witnesses should be of sound mind, and not be named as beneficiaries in the will.

Affidavit of Subscribing Witnesses

STATE OF _Illinois_____ )

                                 ss.:

COUNTY OF ___Cook_____ )

     On _march 11_____, 19_89_, personally appeared before me, the undersigned authority

1. __Sally B. Hill_____  2. ___Mark Collins_____
         Testatrix                                 Witness

3. __Linda Collins_____  4. ___Ralph Collins_____
         Witness                                   Witness

known to me to be the Testatrix and Witnesses, respectively, who being severally sworn state under oath that, all the subscribing witnesses witnessed the execution of the Will of the within named Testatrix on the same date they subscribed this instrument; the Testatrix in their presence, subscribed the Will at the end and at the time of making the subscription declared the instrument to be the Testatrix's Last Will and Testament; at the request of the Testatrix and in the Testatrix's sight and presence and in the sight and presence of each other, all the subscribing witnesses witnessed the execution of the Will by the Testatrix by subscribing their names as witnesses to it; the Testatrix at the time of the execution of the Will, was over the age of 18 years and appeared to them of sound mind, memory and understanding and was in all respects competent to make a Will; and the Testatrix having declared to the said witnesses that she was not under any duress or any undue influence and that she voluntarily executed this will as her free act and deed.

     The subscribing witnesses further state that this affidavit was executed at the request of the Testatrix, and at the time of the execution of this affidavit the original Will, above described, was exhibited to them and they identified it as such Will by their signatures appearing on it as subscribing witnesses.

     The Testatrix states that each witness was and is competent and of a proper age to witness a will and further acknowledges that she has read the within instrument and she affirms that each and every statement made by the subscribing witness is true to her own knowledge.

Severally subscribed,         TESTATRIX: ___Sally B Hill_____
acknowledged and sworn to
before me on _march 11, 1989_    WITNESS: ___Mark Collins_____

___mark Davis_____          WITNESS: ___Linda Collins_____
Notary Public or Person
Authorized to Take Oaths     WITNESS: ___Ralph collins_____

# Instructions for Completing the Affidavit of Subscribing Witnesses

An Affidavit of Subscribing Witnesses (also known as a self-proving affidavit) which is recognized in most states is also included in the will kit. This Affidavit allows you to self-prove your will. A will does not require this affidavit in order for the will to be valid. However, this affidavit may save much time and expense when a will is being probated. A situation in which this might occur is if the witnesses to the will could not be located when the will was being probated. By the will being self-proved, the witnesses will most likely not have to appear in court. A will is self-proved when the Testator (the person who writes the will) and the witnesses to the will, declare that this document is the Testator's will, and that it was properly executed, and sign this affidavit before an officer authorized to administer oaths or a notary public. This affidavit is included in the will and should be used if possible, but again, a will is valid without an affidavit of subscribing witnesses.

If you choose to self-prove your will, use the following instructions:

1. You must sign your will and have it witnessed by three witnesses, and follow the instructions for the execution of a will, as they are given in this book.

2. If there is not an officer authorized to administer oaths or a notary public present at the will signing, you and the witnesses to the will must at a later time, personally appear before such officer or a notary public. All parties must bring proper identification. Advise the officer or notary public that you want to self-prove your will. Ask the officer or notary public if he or she has a form for this purpose. If yes, follow the officer or notary's instructions.

3. If the officer or notary does not have a form, use the Affidavit of Subscribing Witnesses included in this kit.

4. Use the model affidavit of subscribing witnesses as a guide to filling out your affidavit. You and your witnesses should write your names in the spaces designated "Testator" and "witness." The officer or notary will have you swear to the statements made in the affidavit, and to sign your names at the bottom of the affidavit. The officer or notary will date, sign, and place a stamp or seal on the affidavit.

5. At this time, staple the affidavit to the will so that it becomes the last page.

# Last Will and Testament
# of

Frank S. Hill

**I,** Frank S. Hill , presently residing at
1 main Street, Chicago, Illinois ,
being of full age and sound and disposing mind and memory, hereby make, publish and declare this
to be my Last Will and Testament.

FIRST: I hereby revoke any and all Wills and Codicils by me anytime heretofore made.

SECOND: I direct all of my just debts and funeral expenses be paid out of my Estate as soon
as practicable after my death.

THIRD: I am presently married to Sally B. Hill .

FOURTH: I hereby give, devise and bequeath all of my Estate, real, personal
and mixed, of every kind and nature whatsoever and wheresoever situated, to my
beloved wife absolutely and forever.

FIFTH: In the event that my wife shall predecease me, then and in that
event, I give, devise and bequeath my Estate hereinabove mentioned in paragraph "FOURTH"
herein, to my beloved child or children or grandchildren surviving me,
per stirpes.

SIXTH: In the event I am not survived by my wife or any children, or grandchildren, then,
and in such event, I give, devise and bequeath my said Estate
to the following named beneficiary/beneficiaries or their survivor/survivors in equal shares.

a. Allen Singer, 20 Main Street, Chicago, Illinois
Name and address of beneficiary

b. American Cancer Society, Chicago Chapter
Name and address of beneficiary

c. _____
Name and address of beneficiary

d. _____
Name and address of beneficiary

e. _____
Name and address of beneficiary

# Glossary

The numbers on this page correspond to the numbers on the model will on the previous page. Important words are defined, and important aspects of the model will are explained.

1. A Last Will & Testament, known simply as a "Will," is a written declaration of how a person intends his property to be disposed of after his death.

2. The Testator is Frank S. Hill, the person who is writing the will, and who signs and dates the will.

3. A will must have the full name of the Testator. It is important that the spelling and middle initial, if any, are accurate.

4. A will should also have the Testator's address.

5. The Testator must have the mental capacity to make a will.

6. The will revokes or cancels all former wills and codicils. A codicil is used to add to, remove from, or modify the provisions of a will, and must be signed, declared, and witnessed in the same way as a will.

7. Frank is including a provision to pay all of his outstanding bills and funeral expenses.

8. Sally is Frank's wife.

9. ESTATE — An estate is all of the property that a person owns.

10. GIVE, DEVISE, and BEQUEATH — This is the act of giving away your real estate and personal property by will. "Devise" relates to real estate and "bequeath" relates to personal property.

11. Frank leaves everything to his wife, Sally.

12. Predecease — to die before. If a wife predeceases a husband, then she has passed away before him.

13. If Sally passes away before Frank, Frank leaves everything to his children.

14. PER STIRPES — An example of a per stirpes distribution is the following: If Frank S. Hill has 3 children (Beth, Karen, and Susan) and leaves his estate to his 3 children in equal amounts, then under a per stirpes distribution, if Beth passed away before her father (and left two children), then the 1/3 share that Beth would have been entitled to is passed on to her children so that they each get 1/2 of their mother's share.

15. The Beneficiary is the person, persons, and/or organizations to whom you decide to leave all, or part of your estate.

16. If Frank and Sally's children and grandchildren pass away before Frank, then Frank leaves everything to his brother-in-law Allen Singer and the American Cancer Society in equal shares.

17      SEVENTH: I hereby nominate and appoint my beloved wife to be the Executrix of this, my Last Will and Testament, and I direct that no bond or other security shall be required of her in any jurisdiction. If my said wife is unable to serve as Executrix, then I nominate

18      and appoint __Allen Singer__ , Executor/Executrix of this my Last Will and Testament, and I further direct that he/she not be required to post any bond or other security.

EIGHTH: I give to my Executor/Executrix, authority to exercise all the powers,

19      duties, rights and immunities conferred upon fiduciaries by law with full power to sell to mortgage and to lease, and to invest and reinvest all or any part of my Estate on such terms as he/she deems best.

20      IN WITNESS WHEREOF, I hereunto set my hand this ___11___ day of __march__ , 1989.

_Frank S. Hill_____
(SIGN HERE)

Signed, sealed, published and declared by the above named Testator, as and for his Last Will and Testament, in the presence of us, who at his request, in his presence, and in the presence of one another have hereunto subscribed our names as attesting witnesses, the day and year last written above.

21      _Mark Collins_____     residing at     _420 Lincoln Ave._____
                                                  _Chicago, Illinois_____

        _Linda Collins_____     residing at     _420 Lincoln Ave._____
                                                  _Chicago, Illinois_____

        _Ralph Collins_____     residing at     _420 Lincoln Ave._____
                                                  _Chicago, Illinois_____

40

# Glossary

The numbers on this page correspond to the numbers on the model will on the previous page. Important words are defined, and important aspects of the model will are explained.

17. The Executor/Executrix is the person that you name in the will to carry out the terms of your will and to administer the estate. The person writing the will (Testator) often will name the beneficiary of the largest portion of the estate as Executor/Executrix. However, the Executor/Executrix is not legally required to be a beneficiary. Your will form provides that the Executor/Executrix not be required to post a bond for the Court.

18. Frank appoints his wife to settle the affairs of his estate. If Sally is unavailable Frank appoints his brother-in- law Allen Singer.

19. Frank gives Sally total discretion subject to state law to carry out the terms of the will.

20. Frank dates and signs the will in front of the witnesses.

21. The Witnesses are the people who after seeing the Testator sign and date the will and declare that this is his will, witness the will by signing their names and listing their home addresses at the end of the will. The witnesses must be together and see you sign the will. Most states require only 2 witnesses, but some states require 3 witnesses. Your will form includes 3 signature lines for your protection. The witnesses should be of sound mind, and not be named as beneficiaries in the will.

**Affidavit of Subscribing Witnesses**

STATE OF ___Illinois___ )

COUNTY OF ___Cook___ ) ss.:

On ___March 11___, 19_89_, personally appeared before me, the undersigned authority

1. ___Frank S. Hill___
   Testator

2. ___Mark Collins___
   Witness

3. ___Linda Collins___
   Witness

4. ___Ralph Collins___
   Witness

known to me to be the Testator and Witnesses, respectively, who being severally sworn state under oath that, all the subscribing witnesses witnessed the execution of the Will of the within named Testator on the same date they subscribed this instrument; the Testator in their presence, subscribed the Will at the end and at the time of making the subscription declared the instrument to be the Testator's Last Will and Testament; at the request of the Testator and in the Testator's sight and presence and in the sight and presence of each other, all the subscribing witnesses witnessed the execution of the Will by the Testator by subscribing their names as witnesses to it; the Testator at the time of the execution of the Will, was over the age of 18 years and appeared to them of sound mind, memory and understanding and was in all respects competent to make a Will; and the Testator having declared to the said witnesses that he was not under any duress or any undue influence and that he voluntarily executed this will as his free act and deed.

The subscribing witnesses further state that this affidavit was executed at the request of the Testator, and at the time of the execution of this affidavit the original Will, above described, was exhibited to them and they identified it as such Will by their signatures appearing on it as subscribing witnesses.

The Testator states that each witness was and is competent and of a proper age to witness a will and further acknowledges that he has read the within instrument and he affirms that each and every statement made by the subscribing witness is true to his own knowledge.

Severally subscribed,
acknowledged and sworn to
before me on _March 11, 1989_

_Mark Davis_
Notary Public or Person
Authorized to Take Oaths

TESTATOR: _Frank S. Hill_

WITNESS: _Mark Collins_

WITNESS: _Linda Collins_

WITNESS: _Ralph Collins_

# Instructions for Completing the Affidavit of Subscribing Witnesses

An Affidavit of Subscribing Witnesses (also known as a self-proving affidavit) which is recognized in most states is also included in the will kit. This Affidavit allows you to self-prove your will. A will does not require this affidavit in order for the will to be valid. However, this affidavit may save much time and expense when a will is being probated. A situation in which this might occur is if the witnesses to the will could not be located when the will was being probated. By the will being self-proved, the witnesses will most likely not have to appear in court. A will is self-proved when the Testator (the person who writes the will) and the witnesses to the will, declare that this document is the Testator's will, and that it was properly executed, and sign this affidavit before an officer authorized to administer oaths or a notary public. This affidavit is included in the will and should be used if possible, but again, a will is valid without an affidavit of subscribing witnesses.

If you choose to self-prove your will, use the following instructions:

1. You must sign your will and have it witnessed by three witnesses, and follow the instructions for the execution of a will, as they are given in this book.

2. If there is not an officer authorized to administer oaths or a notary public present at the will signing, you and the witnesses to the will must at a later time personally appear before such officer or a notary public. All parties must bring proper identification. Advise the officer or notary public that you want to self-prove your will. Ask the officer or notary public if he or she has a form for this purpose. If yes, follow the officer or notary's instructions.

3. If the officer or notary does not have a form, use the Affidavit of Subscribing Witnesses included in this kit.

4. Use the model affidavit of subscribing witnesses as a guide to filling out your affidavit. You and your witnesses should write your names in the spaces designated "Testator" and "witness." The officer or notary will have you swear to the statements made in the affidavit, and to sign your names at the bottom of the affidavit. The officer or notary will date, sign, and place a stamp or seal on the affidavit.

5. At this time, staple the affidavit to the will so that it becomes the last page.

# Last Will and Testament
## of

2 _____Roger T. Smith_____

3 **I,** _____Roger T. Smith_____, presently residing at

4 _2 River Ave., San Francisco, California_ ,

5 being of full age and sound and disposing mind and memory, hereby make, publish and declare this to be my Last Will and Testament.

6       FIRST: I hereby revoke any and all Wills and Codicils by me anytime heretofore made.

7       SECOND: I direct all of my just debts and funeral expenses be paid out of my Estate as soon as practicable after my death.

8       THIRD:     a. I am presently not married.
               b. I am the parent of the following child/children:

1. _Stanley Smith_     2. _Edna Smith_

3. _Barry Smith_     4. _____

5. _____     6. _____

9       FOURTH: I hereby give, devise and bequeath all of my Estate, real, personal and mixed,

10, 11   of every kind and nature whatsoever and wheresoever situated, to my beloved child or

12   children or grandchildren surviving me, per stirpes.

      FIFTH: I nominate and appoint _Carol Brown_, as

13 Executor/Executrix of this Will. In the event he/she shall predecease me or fails to serve as such Executor/Executrix, then in such event, I nominate and appoint

14 _Joyce Brown_, Executor/Executrix of this my Last Will and Testament. I further direct that no appointee hereunder shall be required to give any bond for the faithful performance of his/her duties.

      SIXTH: In the event that any child/children of mine shall be minors at my death and

15 shall not be survived by their natural parent, I then nominate and appoint
_Carol Brown_ as Guardian of the person and property of my

16 minor child/children. In the event that _Carol Brown_ shall be unable or unwilling to serve as Guardian, then, and in such event I nominate and appoint

17 _Joyce Brown_ Guardian of the person and property of my minor child or children, and I direct that no bond shall be required of any Guardian herein.

# Glossary

The numbers on this page correspond to the numbers on the model will on the previous page. Important words are defined, and important aspects of the model will are explained.

1. A Last Will & Testament, known simply as a "Will," is a written declaration of how a person intends his property to be disposed of after his death.

2. The Testator is Roger T. Smith, the person who is writing the will, and who signs and dates the will.

3. A will must have the full name of the Testator. It is important that the spelling and middle initial, if any, are accurate.

4. A will should also have the Testator's address.

5. The Testator must have the mental capacity to make a will.

6. The will revokes or cancels all former wills and codicils. A codicil is used to add to, remove from or modify the provisions of a will, and must be signed, declared and witnessed in the same way as a will.

7. Roger is including a provision to pay all of his outstanding bills and funeral expenses.

8. Roger is not married and is the father of three children.

9. ESTATE — An estate is all of the property that a person owns.

10. GIVE, DEVISE, and BEQUEATH — This is the act of giving away your real estate and personal property by will. "Devise" relates to real estate and "bequeath" relates to personal property.

11. Roger leaves everything to his children.

12. PER STIRPES — An example of a per stirpes distribution is the following: If Roger T. Smith has 3 children (Sally, Edna, and Barry) and leaves his estate to his 3 children in equal amounts, then under a per stirpes distribution, if Edna passed away before her father (and left two children), then the 1/3 share that Edna would have been entitled to is passed on to her children so that they each get 1/2 of their mother's share.

13. The Executor/Executrix is the person that you name in the will to carry out the terms of your will and to administer the estate. The person writing the will (Testator) often will name the beneficiary of the largest portion of the estate as Executor/Executrix. However, the Executor/Executrix is not legally required to be a beneficiary. Your will form provides that the Executor/Executrix not be required to post a bond for the Court.

14. Roger appoints Carol Brown to settle the affairs of his estate. If Carol is unavailable Roger appoints Joyce Brown.

15. The Guardian/Co-guardians — the person whom you choose to be legally responsible for the care of your minor children and their property.

16. The minor child/children — children who are not yet of legal age.

17. Roger appoints Carol Brown to be the guardian of his minor children. If Carol is unavailable, Roger appoints Joyce Brown.

18         SEVENTH: I give to my Executor/Executrix, the authority to exercise all the powers, duties, rights and immunities conferred upon fiduciaries by law with full power to sell to mortgage and to lease, and to invest and reinvest all or any part of my Estate on such terms as he/she deems best.

19         IN WITNESS WHEREOF, I hereunto set my hand this _____*11*_____ day of _____*March*_____, 19*89*.

*Roger S. Smith*
(SIGN HERE)

Signed, sealed, published and declared by the above named Testator, as and for his Last Will and Testament, in the presence of us, who at his request, in his presence, and in the presence of one another have hereunto subscribed our names as attesting witnesses, the day and year last written above.

20    *Sol Grun*     residing at     *10 Hall Place*
                                                    *San Francisco, CA*

   *Heidi Grun*     residing at     *10 Hall Place*
                                                    *San Francisco, CA*

   *Tom Brown*     residing at     *27 Center Ave.*
                                                    *San Francisco, CA*

# Glossary

The numbers on this page correspond to the numbers on the model will on the previous page. Important words are defined, and important aspects of the model will are explained.

18. Roger gives Carol total discretion subject to state law to carry out the terms of the will.

19. Roger dates and signs the will in front of the witnesses.

20. The Witnesses are the people who after seeing the Testator sign and date the will and declare that this is his will, witness the will by signing their names and listing their home addresses at the end of the will. The witnesses must be together and see you sign the will. Most states require only 2 witnesses, but some states require 3 witnesses. Your will form includes 3 signature lines for your protection. The witnesses should be of sound mind, and not be named as beneficiaries in the will.

Affidavit of Subscribing Witnesses

STATE OF _California_ )
                                              ss.:
COUNTY OF _San Francisco_ )

On _march 11_ ,19_89_ ,personally appeared before me, the undersigned authority

1. _Roger T. Smith_          2. _Sol Green_
        Testator                          Witness

3. _Heidi Green_             4. _Tom Brown_
        Witness                          Witness

known to me to be the Testator and Witnesses, respectively, who being severally sworn state under oath that, all the subscribing witnesses witnessed the execution of the Will of the within named Testator on the same date they subscribed this instrument; the Testator in their presence, subscribed the Will at the end and at the time of making the subscription declared the instrument to be the Testator's Last Will and Testament; at the request of the Testator and in the Testator's sight and presence and in the sight and presence of each other, all the subscribing witnesses witnessed the execution of the Will by the Testator by subscribing their names as witnesses to it; the Testator at the time of the execution of the Will, was over the age of 18 years and appeared to them of sound mind, memory and understanding and was in all respects competent to make a Will; and the Testator having declared to the said witnesses that he was not under any duress or any undue influence and that he voluntarily executed this will.

The subscribing witnesses further state that this affidavit was executed at the request of the Testator, and at the time of the execution of this affidavit the original Will, above described, was exhibited to them and they identified it as such Will by their signatures appearing on it as subscribing witnesses.

The Testator states that each witness was and is competent and of a proper age to witness a will and further acknowledges that he has read the within instrument and he affirms that each and every statement made by the subscribing witness is true to his own knowledge.

Severally subscribed,                    TESTATOR: _Roger J. Smith_
acknowledged and sworn to
before me on _march 11, 1989_            WITNESS: _Sol Green_

_Mark Davis_                             WITNESS: _Heidi Green_
Notary Public or Person
Authorized to Take Oaths                 WITNESS: _Tom Brown_

# Instructions for Completing the Affidavit of Subscribing Witnesses

An Affidavit of Subscribing Witnesses (also known as a self-proving affidavit) which is recognized in most states is also included in the will kit. This Affidavit allows you to self-prove your will. A will does not require this affidavit in order for the will to be valid. However, this affidavit may save much time and expense when a will is being probated. A situation in which this might occur is if the witnesses to the will could not be located when the will was being probated. By the will being self-proved, the witnesses will most likely not have to appear in court. A will is self-proved when the Testator (the person who writes the will) and the witnesses to the will, declare that this document is the Testator's will, and that it was properly executed, and sign this affidavit before an officer authorized to administer oaths or a notary public. This affidavit is included in the will and should be used if possible, but again, a will is valid without an affidavit of subscribing witnesses.

If you choose to self-prove your will, use the following instructions:

1. You must sign your will and have it witnessed by three witnesses, and follow the instructions for the execution of a will, as they are given in this book.

2. If there is not an officer authorized to administer oaths or a notary public present at the will signing, you and the witnesses to the will must at a later time personally appear before such officer or a notary public. All parties must bring proper identification. Advise the officer or notary public that you want to self-prove your will. Ask the officer or notary public if he or she has a form for this purpose. If yes, follow the officer or notary's instructions.

3. If the officer or notary does not have a form, use the Affidavit of Subscribing Witnesses included in this kit.

4. Use the model affidavit of subscribing witnesses as a guide to filling out your affidavit. You and your witnesses should write your names in the spaces designated "Testator" and "witness." The officer or notary will have you swear to the statements made in the affidavit, and to sign your names at the bottom of the affidavit. The officer or notary will date, sign, and place a stamp or seal on the affidavit.

5. At this time, staple the affidavit to the will so that it becomes the last page.

# Last Will and Testament
## of

**2** _____Judith S. Jacobs_____

**3** **I,** ___Judith S. Jacobs___ , presently residing at

**4** ___15 Water Street, Miami, Florida___ ,

**5** being of full age and sound and disposing mind and memory, hereby make, publish and declare this to be my Last Will and Testament.

**6**       FIRST: I hereby revoke any and all Wills and Codicils by me anytime heretofore made.

**7**       SECOND: I direct all of my just debts and funeral expenses be paid out of my Estate as soon as practicable after my death.

**8**       THIRD:     a. I am presently not married.
                    b. I am the parent of the following child/children:

1. ___Steven Jacobs___     2. ___Randy Jacobs___
3. ___David Jacobs___     4. _____
5. _____     6. _____

**9**       FOURTH: I hereby give, devise and bequeath all of my Estate, real, personal and mixed,
**10, 11** of every kind and nature whatsoever and wheresoever situated, to my beloved child or
**12** children or grandchildren surviving me, per stirpes.

      FIFTH: I nominate and appoint ___Steven Jacobs___ , as
**13** Executor/Executrix of this Will. In the event he/she shall predecease me or fails to serve as such Executor/Executrix, then in such event, I nominate and appoint

**14** ___Randy Jacobs___ , Executor/Executrix of this my Last Will and Testament. I further direct that no appointee hereunder shall be required to give any bond for the faithful performance of his/her duties.

**15**       SIXTH: I give to my Executor/Executrix, the authority to exercise all the powers, duties, rights and immunities conferred upon fiduciaries by law with full power to sell to mortgage and to lease, and to invest and reinvest all or any part of my Estate on such terms as he/she deems best.

# Glossary

The numbers on this page correspond to the numbers on the model will on the previous page. Important words are defined, and important aspects of the model will are explained.

1. A Last Will & Testament, known simply as a "Will," is a written declaration of how a person intends his property to be disposed of after his death.

2. The Testatrix is Judith S. Jacobs, the person who is writing the will, and who signs and dates the will.

3. A will must have the full name of the Testatrix. It is important that the spelling and middle initial, if any, are accurate.

4. A will should also have the Testatrix's address.

5. The Testatrix must have the mental capacity to make a will.

6. The will revokes or cancels all former wills and codicils. A codicil is used to add to, remove from or modify the provisions of a will, and must be signed, declared and witnessed in the same way as a will.

7. Judith is including a provision to pay all of her outstanding bills and funeral expenses.

8. Judith is not married and is the mother of three children.

9. Estate — An estate is all of the property that a person owns.

10. Give, devise, and bequeath — This is the act of giving away your real estate and personal property by will. "Devise" relates to real estate and "bequeath" relates to personal property.

11. Judith leaves everything to her children.

12. Per stirpes — An example of a per stirpes distribution is the following: If Judith S. Jacobs has 3 children (Steven, Randy, and David) and leaves her estate to her 3 children in equal amounts, then under a per stirpes distribution, if Randy passed away before his mother (and left two children), then the 1/3 share that Randy would have been entitled to is passed on to his children so that they each get 1/2 of their father's share.

13. The Executor/Executrix is the person that you name in the will to carry out the terms of your will and to administer the estate. The person writing the will (Testatrix) often will name the beneficiary of the largest portion of the estate as Executor/Executrix. However, the Executor/Executrix is not legally required to be a beneficiary. Your will form provides that the Executor/Executrix not be required to post a bond for the Court.

14. Judith appoints Steven Jacobs to settle the affairs of her estate. If Steven is unavailable, Judith appoints Randy Jacobs.

15. Judith gives Steven total discretion subject to state law to carry out the terms of the will.

16       IN WITNESS WHEREOF, I hereunto set my hand this _____11_____ day of
_march_____ , 19_89_.

_____Judith S Jacobs_____
(SIGN HERE)

      Signed, sealed, published and declared by the above named Testatrix, as and for her Last Will and Testament, in the presence of us, who at her request, in her presence, and in the presence of one another have hereunto subscribed our names as attesting witnesses, the day and year last written above.

17     _Carolyn Jones_     residing at     _800 Collins Avenue_
                                            _Miami, Florida_

    _Harry Jones_     residing at     _800 Collins Avenue_
                                            _Miami, Florida_

    _Robert Jones_     residing at     _800 Collins Avenue_
                                            _Miami, Florida_

# Glossary

The numbers on this page correspond to the numbers on the model will on the previous page. Important words are defined, and important aspects of the model will are explained.

16. Judith dates and signs the will in front of the witnesses.

17. The Witnesses are the people who after seeing the Testatrix sign and date the will and declare that this is her will, witness the will by signing their names and listing their home addresses at the end of the will. The witnesses must be together and see you sign the will. Most states require only 2 witnesses, but some states require 3 witnesses. Your will form includes 3 signature lines for your protection. The witnesses should be of sound mind, and not be named as beneficiaries in the will.

**Affidavit of Subscribing Witnesses**

STATE OF _____Florida_____ )

                            **ss.:**

COUNTY OF _____Dade_____ )

          On _____March 11_____ , 19_89_ , personally appeared before me, the undersigned authority

| | |
|---|---|
| 1. ___Judith S. Jacobs___ <br> Testatrix | 2. ___Carolyn Jones___ <br> Witness |
| 3. ___Harry Jones___ <br> Witness | 4. ___Robert Jones___ <br> Witness |

known to me to be the Testatrix and Witnesses, respectively, who being severally sworn state under oath that, all the subscribing witnesses witnessed the execution of the Will of the within named Testatrix on the same date they subscribed this instrument; the Testatrix in their presence, subscribed the Will at the end and at the time of making the subscription declared the instrument to be the Testatrix's Last Will and Testament; at the request of the Testatrix and in the Testatrix's sight and presence and in the sight and presence of each other, all the subscribing witnesses witnessed the execution of the Will by the Testatrix by subscribing their names as witnesses to it; the Testatrix at the time of the execution of the Will, was over the age of 18 years and appeared to them of sound mind, memory and understanding and was in all respects competent to make a Will; and the Testatrix having declared to the said witnesses that she was not under any duress or any undue influence and that she voluntarily executed this will as his free act and deed.

        The subscribing witnesses further state that this affidavit was executed at the request of the Testatrix, and at the time of the execution of this affidavit the original Will, above described, was exhibited to them and they identified it as such Will by their signatures appearing on it as subscribing witnesses.

        The Testatrix states that each witness was and is competent and of a proper age to witness a will and further acknowledges that she has read the within instrument and she affirms that each and every statement made by the subscribing witness is true to her own knowledge.

Severally subscribed,           TESTATRIX: _Judith S. Jacobs_
acknowledged and sworn to
before me on _March 11, 1989_     WITNESS: _Carolyn Jones_

                                     WITNESS: _Harry Jones_

_Mark Davis_
Notary Public or Person         WITNESS: _Robert Jones_
Authorized to Take Oaths

# Instructions for Completing the Affidavit of Subscribing Witnesses

An Affidavit of Subscribing Witnesses (also known as a self-proving affidavit) which is recognized in most states is also included in the will kit. This Affidavit allows you to self-prove your will. A will does not require this affidavit in order for the will to be valid. However, this affidavit may save much time and expense when a will is being probated. A situation in which this might occur is if the witnesses to the will could not be located when the will was being probated. By the will being self-proved, the witnesses will most likely not have to appear in court. A will is self-proved when the Testator (the person who writes the will) and the witnesses to the will, declare that this document is the Testator's will, and that it was properly executed, and sign this affidavit before an officer authorized to administer oaths or a notary public. This affidavit is included in the will and should be used if possible, but again, a will is valid without an affidavit of subscribing witnesses.

If you choose to self-prove your will, use the following instructions:

1. You must sign your will and have it witnessed by three witnesses, and follow the instructions for the execution of a will, as they are given in this book.

2. If there is not an officer authorized to administer oaths or a notary public present at the will signing, you and the witnesses to the will must at a later time personally appear before such officer or a notary public. All parties must bring proper identification. Advise the officer or notary public that you want to self-prove your will. Ask the officer or notary public if he or she has a form for this purpose. If yes, follow the officer or notary's instructions.

3. If the officer or notary does not have a form, use the Affidavit of Subscribing Witnesses included in this kit.

4. Use the model affidavit of subscribing witnesses as a guide to filling out your affidavit. You and your witnesses should write your names in the spaces designated "Testator" and "witness." The officer or notary will have you swear to the statements made in the affidavit, and to sign your names at the bottom of the affidavit. The officer or notary will date, sign, and place a stamp or seal on the affidavit.

5. At this time, staple the affidavit to the will so that it becomes the last page.

# Last Will and Testament
## of

Robert Murray

I, Robert Murray , presently residing at

27 Astor Place, Detroit, Michigan ,

being of full age and sound and disposing mind and memory, hereby make, publish and declare this to be my Last Will and Testament.

FIRST: I hereby revoke any and all Wills and Codicils by me anytime heretofore made.

SECOND: I direct that all of my just debts and funeral expenses be paid out of my Estate as soon as practicable after my death.

THIRD: I am presently not married.

FOURTH: I hereby give, devise and bequeath all of my Estate, real, personal and mixed, of every kind and nature whatsoever and wheresoever situated, to

Larry Adams .

FIFTH: In the event that I am not survived by Larry Adams ,

I give, devise and bequeath my said estate to Paul Andrews .

SIXTH: I nominate and appoint Larry Adams ,

as Executor/Executrix of this Will. In the even he/she shall predecease me or fails to serve as such Executor/Executrix, then in such event, I nominate and appoint

Paul Andrews , Executor/Executrix of this my Last Will and Testament. I further direct that no appointee hereunder shall be required to give any bond for the faithful performance of his/her duties.

SEVENTH: I give to my Executor/Executrix, authority to exercise all the powers, duties, rights and immunities conferred upon fiduciaries by law with full power to sell to mortgage and to lease, and to invest and reinvest all or any part of my Estate on such terms as he/she deems best.

# Glossary

The numbers on this page correspond to the numbers on the model will on the previous page. Important words are defined, and important aspects of the model will are explained.

1. A Last Will & Testament, known simply as a "Will," is a written declaration of how a person intends his property to be disposed of after his death.

2. The Testator is Robert Murray, the person who is writing the will, and who signs and dates the will.

3. A will must have the full name of the Testator. It is important that the spelling and middle initial, if any, are accurate.

4. A will should also have the Testator's address.

5. The Testator must have the mental capacity to make a will.

6. The will revokes or cancels all former wills and codicils. A codicil is used to add to, remove from or modify the provisions of a will, and must be signed, declared and witnessed in the same way as a will.

7. Robert is including a provision to pay all of his outstanding bills and funeral expenses.

8. Robert is not married.

9. Estate — An estate is all of the property that a person owns.

10. Give, devise, and bequeath — This is the act of giving away your real estate and personal property by will. "Devise" relates to real estate and "bequeath" relates to personal property.

11. Robert leaves everything to his friend Larry Adams.

12. The Executor/Executrix is the person that you name in the will to carry out the terms of your will and to administer the estate. The person writing the will (Testator) often will name the beneficiary of the largest portion of the estate as Executor/Executrix. However, the Executor/Executrix is not legally required to be a beneficiary. Your will form provides that the Executor/Executrix not be required to post a bond for the Court.

13. Robert appoints Larry Adams to settle the affairs of his estate.

14. If Larry is unavailable Robert appoints Paul Andrews.

15. Robert gives Larry total discretion subject to state law to carry out the terms of the will.

16  IN WITNESS WHEREOF, I hereunto set my hand this _____11_____ day of
_march_____ , 19_89_.

_____Robert Murray_____
(SIGN HERE)

Signed, sealed, published and declared by the above named Testator, as and for his Last Will and Testament, in the presence of us, who at his request, in his presence, and in the presence of one another have hereunto subscribed our names as attesting witnesses, the day and year last written above.

17  _____Rosalind Bell_____  residing at  _25 Central Avenue._
_Detroit, Michigan_

_____Samuel Bell_____  residing at  _25 Central Avenue_
_Detroit, Michigan_

_____Steven Crane_____  residing at  _50 Central Ave._
_Detroit, Michigan_

# Glossary

The numbers on this page correspond to the numbers on the model will on the previous page. Important words are defined, and important aspects of the model will are explained.

16. Robert dates and signs the will in front of the witnesses.

17. The Witnesses are the people who after seeing the Testator sign and date the will and declare that this is his will, witness the will by signing their names and listing their home addresses at the end of the will. The witnesses must be together and see you sign the will. Most states require only 2 witnesses, but some states require 3 witnesses. Your will form includes 3 signature lines for your protection. The witnesses should be of sound mind, and not be named as beneficiaries in the will.

Affidavit of Subscribing Witnesses

STATE OF _____Michigan_____ )
                                        ss.:
COUNTY OF _____Wayne_____ )

On _____March 11_____ ,19_89_ , personally appeared before me, the undersigned authority

1._____Robert Murray_____
        Testator

2._____Rosalind Bell_____
        Witness

3._____Samuel Bell_____
        Witness

4._____Steven Crane_____
        Witness

known to me to be the Testator and Witnesses, respectively, who being severally sworn state under oath that, all the subscribing witnesses witnessed the execution of the Will of the within named Testator on the same date they subscribed this instrument; the Testator in their presence, subscribed the Will at the end and at the time of making the subscription declared the instrument to be the Testator's Last Will and Testament; at the request of the Testator and in the Testator's sight and presence and in the sight and presence of each other, all the subscribing witnesses witnessed the execution of the Will by the Testator by subscribing their names as witnesses to it; the Testator at the time of the execution of the Will, was over the age of 18 years and appeared to them of sound mind, memory and understanding and was in all respects competent to make a Will; and the Testator having declared to the said witnesses that he was not under any duress or any undue influence and that he voluntarily executed this will as his free act and deed.

The subscribing witnesses further state that this affidavit was executed at the request of the Testator, and at the time of the execution of this affidavit the original Will, above described, was exhibited to them and they identified it as such Will by their signatures appearing on it as subscribing witnesses.

The Testator states that each witness was and is competent and of a proper age to witness a will and further acknowledges that he has read the within instrument and he affirms that each and every statement made by the subscribing witness is true to his own knowledge.

Severally subscribed,
acknowledged and sworn to
before me on _march 11, 1989_

_Mark Davis_
Notary Public or Person
Authorized to Take Oaths

TESTATOR: _Robert Murray_

WITNESS: _Rosalind Bell_

WITNESS: _Samuel Bell_

WITNESS: _Steven Crane_

# Instructions for Completing the Affidavit of Subscribing Witnesses

An Affidavit of Subscribing Witnesses (also known as a self-proving affidavit) which is recognized in most states is also included in the will kit. This Affidavit allows you to self-prove your will. A will does not require this affidavit in order for the will to be valid. However, this affidavit may save much time and expense when a will is being probated. A situation in which this might occur is if the witnesses to the will could not be located when the will was being probated. By the will being self-proved, the witnesses will most likely not have to appear in court. A will is self-proved when the Testator (the person who writes the will) and the witnesses to the will, declare that this document is the Testator's will, and that it was properly executed, and sign this affidavit before an officer authorized to administer oaths or a notary public. This affidavit is included in the will and should be used if possible, but again, a will is valid without an affidavit of subscribing witnesses.

If you choose to self-prove your will, use the following instructions:

1. You must sign your will and have it witnessed by three witnesses, and follow the instructions for the execution of a will, as they are given in this book.

2. If there is not an officer authorized to administer oaths or a notary public present at the will signing, you and the witnesses to the will must at a later time personally appear before such officer or a notary public. All parties must bring proper identification. Advise the officer or notary public that you want to self-prove your will. Ask the officer or notary public if he or she has a form for this purpose. If yes, follow the officer or notary's instructions.

3. If the officer or notary does not have a form, use the Affidavit of Subscribing Witnesses included in this kit.

4. Use the model affidavit of subscribing witnesses as a guide to filling out your affidavit. You and your witnesses should write your names in the spaces designated "Testator" and "witness." The officer or notary will have you swear to the statements made in the affidavit, and to sign your names at the bottom of the affidavit. The officer or notary will date, sign, and place a stamp or seal on the affidavit.

5. At this time, staple the affidavit to the will so that it becomes the last page.

# Last Will and Testament

## of

2    _____Eric Carter_____

3    **I**, ___Eric Carter_____ , presently residing at

4    ___555 Center Street, Dallas, Texas_____ ,

5    being of full age and sound and disposing mind and memory, hereby make, publish and declare this to be my Last Will and Testament.

6         FIRST: I hereby revoke any and all Wills and Codicils by me anytime heretofore made.

7         SECOND: I direct that all of my just debts and funeral expenses be paid out of my Estate as soon as practicable after my death.

8         THIRD: I am presently not married.

9         FOURTH: I hereby give, devise and bequeath all of my Estate, real, personal
10   and mixed, of every kind and nature whatsoever and wheresoever situated, to the following
11   names beneficiaries or their survivors in equal shares.

12   a. _Rose Carter, 1 Spruce Street, Dallas, Texas_____
Name and address of beneficiary

b. _Michael Carter, 1 Spruce Street, Dallas, Texas_____
Name and address of beneficiary

c. _____
Name and address of beneficiary

d. _____
Name and address of beneficiary

e. _____
Name and address of beneficiary

13        FIFTH: I nominate and appoint ___Rose Carter_____ ,
as Executor/Executrix of this Will. In the even he/she shall predecease me or fails to serve as such
14   Executor/Executrix, then in such event, I nominate and appoint _Michael Carter_ ,
Executor/Executrix of this my Last Will and Testament. I further direct that no appointee
hereunder shall be required to give any bond for the faithful performance of his/her duties.

# Glossary

The numbers on this page correspond to the numbers on the model will on the previous page. Important words are defined, and important aspects of the model will are explained.

1. A Last Will & Testament, known simply as a "Will," is a written declaration of how a person intends his property to be disposed of after his death.

2. The Testator is Eric Carter, the person who is writing the will, and who signs and dates the will.

3. A will must have the full name of the Testator. It is important that the spelling and middle initial, if any, are accurate.

4. A will should also have the Testator's address.

5. The Testator must have the mental capacity to make a will.

6. The will revokes or cancels all former wills and codicils. A codicil is used to add to, remove from or modify the provisions of a will, and must be signed, declared and witnessed in the same way as a will.

7. Eric is including a provision to pay all of his outstanding bills and funeral expenses.

8. Eric is not married.

9. Estate — An estate is all of the property that a person owns.

10. Give, devise, and bequeath — This is the act of giving away your real estate and personal property by will. "Devise" relates to real estate and "bequeath" relates to personal property.

11. The Beneficiary is the person, persons and/or organizations to whom you decide to leave all or part of your estate.

12. Eric leaves everything to his mother and father in equal shares. Eric did not have to name a relative. Eric could have named a friend, friends, other relatives, or organizations such as a church.

13. The Executor/Executrix is the person that you name in the will to carry out the terms of your will and to administer the estate. The person writing the will (Testator) often will name the beneficiary of the largest portion of the estate as Executor/Executrix. However, the Executor/Executrix is not legally required to be a beneficiary. Your will form provides that the Executor/Executrix not be required to post a bond for the Court.

14. Eric appoints his mother to settle the affairs of his estate. If his mother is unavailable Eric appoints his father.

15      SIXTH: I give to my Executor/Executrix, the authority to exercise all the powers, duties, rights and immunities conferred upon fiduciaries by law with full power to sell to mortgage and to lease, and to invest and reinvest all or any part of my Estate on such terms as he/she deems best.

16      IN WITNESS WHEREOF, I hereunto set my hand this _____11_____ day of ___march_____ , 19_89_.

*Eric Carter*

(SIGN HERE)

Signed, sealed, published and declared by the above named Testator, as and for his Last Will and Testament, in the presence of us, who at his request, in his presence, and in the presence of one another have hereunto subscribed our names as attesting witnesses, the day and year last written above.

17      _Nick Reid_____      residing at    _36 Chambers St._
                                            _Dallas, Texas_

        _Barry Black_____    residing at    _365 Bowery Ave._
                                            _Dallas, Texas_

        _Wilma Black_____    residing at    _365 Bowery Ave._
                                            _Dallas, Texas_

# Glossary

The numbers on this page correspond to the numbers on the model will on the previous page. Important words are defined, and important aspects of the model will are explained.

15. Eric gives his mother total discretion subject to state law to carry out the terms of the will.

16. Eric dates and signs the will in front of the witnesses.

17. The Witnesses are the people who after seeing the Testator sign and date the will and declare that this is his will, witness the will by signing their names and listing their home addresses at the end of the will. The witnesses must be together and see you sign the will. Most states require only 2 witnesses, but some states require 3 witnesses. Your will form includes 3 signature lines for your protection. The witnesses should be of sound mind, and not be named as beneficiaries in the will.

**Affidavit of Subscribing Witnesses**

STATE OF _____Texas_____ )

COUNTY OF _____Dallas_____ )   ss.:

        On _____March 11_____, 19_89_, personally appeared before me, the undersigned authority

1. _____Eric Carter_____      2. _____Nick Reid_____
        Testator                             Witness

3. _____Barry Black_____      4. _____Wilma Black_____
        Witness                             Witness

known to me to be the Testator and Witnesses, respectively, who being severally sworn state under oath that, all the subscribing witnesses witnessed the execution of the Will of the within named Testator on the same date they subscribed this instrument; the Testator in their presence, subscribed the Will at the end and at the time of making the subscription declared the instrument to be the Testator's Last Will and Testament; at the request of the Testator and in the Testator's sight and presence and in the sight and presence of each other, all the subscribing witnesses witnessed the execution of the Will by the Testator by subscribing their names as witnesses to it; the Testator at the time of the execution of the Will, was over the age of 18 years and appeared to them of sound mind, memory and understanding and was in all respects competent to make a Will; and the Testator having declared to the said witnesses that he was not under any duress or any undue influence and that he voluntarily executed this will as his free act and deed.

        The subscribing witnesses further state that this affidavit was executed at the request of the Testator, and at the time of the execution of this affidavit the original Will, above described, was exhibited to them and they identified it as such Will by their signatures appearing on it as subscribing witnesses.

        The Testator states that each witness was and is competent and of a proper age to witness a will and further acknowledges that he has read the within instrument and he affirms that each and every statement made by the subscribing witness is true to his own knowledge.

Severally subscribed,          TESTATOR: _____Eric Carter_____
acknowledged and sworn to
before me on _March 11, 1989_      WITNESS: _____Barry Black_____

_____Mark Davis_____           WITNESS: _____Nick Reid_____
Notary Public or Person
Authorized to Take Oaths       WITNESS: _____Wilma Black_____

# Instructions for Completing the Affidavit of Subscribing Witnesses

An Affidavit of Subscribing Witnesses (also known as a self-proving affidavit) which is recognized in most states is also included in the will kit. This Affidavit allows you to self-prove your will. A will does not require this affidavit in order for the will to be valid. However, this affidavit may save much time and expense when a will is being probated. A situation in which this might occur is if the witnesses to the will could not be located when the will was being probated. By the will being self-proved, the witnesses will most likely not have to appear in court. A will is self-proved when the Testator (the person who writes the will) and the witnesses to the will, declare that this document is the Testator's will, and that it was properly executed, and sign this affidavit before an officer authorized to administer oaths or a notary public. This affidavit is included in the will and should be used if possible, but again, a will is valid without an affidavit of subscribing witnesses.

If you choose to self-prove your will, use the following instructions:

1. You must sign your will and have it witnessed by three witnesses, and follow the instructions for the execution of a will, as they are given in this book.

2. If there is not an officer authorized to administer oaths or a notary public present at the will signing, you and the witnesses to the will must at a later time, personally appear before such officer or a notary public. All parties must bring proper identification. Advise the officer or notary public that you want to self-prove your will. Ask the officer or notary public if he or she has a form for this purpose. If yes, follow the officer or notary's instructions.

3. If the officer or notary does not have a form, use the Affidavit of Subscribing Witnesses included in this kit.

4. Use the model affidavit of subscribing witnesses as a guide to filling out your affidavit. You and your witnesses should write your names in the spaces designated "Testator" and "witness." The officer or notary will have you swear to the statements made in the affidavit, and to sign your names at the bottom of the affidavit. The officer or notary will date, sign, and place a stamp or seal on the affidavit.

5. At this time, staple the affidavit to the will so that it becomes the last page.

# Last Will and Testament
# of

2    _____Jean Campbell_____

3    **I**, _____Jean Campbell_____ , presently residing at

4    _____2630 Grand Street, Philadelphia, PA_____ ,

5    being of full age and sound and disposing mind and memory, hereby make, publish and declare this to be my Last Will and Testament.

6    FIRST: I hereby revoke any and all Wills and Codicils by me anytime heretofore made.

7    SECOND: I direct all of my just debts and funeral expenses be paid out of my Estate as soon as practicable after my death.

8    THIRD: I hereby nominate and appoint _____Larry Campbell_____ . as Executor/Executrix of this, my Last Will and Testament, and I direct that no bond or other security shall be required of him/her in any jurisdiction. If my said Executor/Executrix hereinabove named is unable to serve as Executor/Executrix then I nominate and appoint

9    _____Mildred Turner_____ , Executor/Executrix of this my Last Will and Testament, and I further direct that he/she not be required to post any bond or other security.

10   FOURTH: I hereby nominate and appoint _____Larry Campbell_____

11   as Guardian of the person and property of my minor children. In the event that said Guardian hereinabove named shall be unable to serve as Guardian, then, and in such event I nominate

12   and appoint _____Mildred Turner_____ , Guardian/Co-guardians of the person and property of my minor child or children, and I direct that no bond shall be required of any Guardian herein.

13   FIFTH: I give to my Executor/Executrix, authority to exercise all the powers, duties, rights and immunities conferred upon fiduciaries by law with full power to sell to mortgage and to lease, and to invest and reinvest all or any part of my Estate on such terms as he/she deems best.

14   SIXTH:

I hereby give, devise and bequeath my entire estate to my husband Larry Campbell, except for the following specific bequests: I give $1,000.00 to the American Cancer Society, Philadelphia Chapter. I give my antique watch to my sister Julie Brown. I give $500.00 to my nephew Martin Davis. If my husband shall die before me, then with the exception of the above bequests, I leave my entire estate to my son Rodney Campbell.

_____68_____

# Glossary

The numbers on this page correspond to the numbers on the model will on the previous page. Important words are defined, and important aspects of the model will are explained.

1. A Last Will & Testament, known simply as a "Will," is a written declaration of how a person intends his property to be disposed of after his death.

2. The Testatrix is Jean Campbell, the person who is writing the will, and who signs and dates the will.

3. A will must have the full name of the Testatrix. It is important that the spelling and middle initial, if any, are accurate.

4. A will should also have the Testatrix's address.

5. The Testatrix must have the mental capacity to make a will.

6. The will revokes or cancels all former wills and codicils. A codicil is used to add to, remove from or modify the provisions of a will, and must be signed, declared and witnessed in the same way as a will.

7. Jean is including a provision to pay all of her outstanding bills and funeral expenses.

8. The Executor/Executrix is the person that you name in the will to carry out the terms of your will and to administer the estate. The person writing the will (Testatrix) often will name the beneficiary of the largest portion of the estate as Executor/Executrix. However, the Executor/Executrix is not legally required to be a beneficiary. Your will form provides that the Executor/Executrix not be required to post a bond for the Court.

9. Jean appoints Larry Campbell to settle the affairs of her estate. If Larry is unavailable Jean appoints Mildred Turner.

10. The Guardian/Co-guardians — the persons whom you choose to be legally responsible for the care of your minor children and their property.

11. The Minor child/children — children who are not yet of legal age.

12. Jean appoints Larry Campbell to be the guardian of her minor children. If Larry is unavailable, Jean appoints Mildred Turner.

13. Jean gives Larry total discretion subject to state law to carry out the terms of the will.

14. Jean leaves her estate to her husband Larry Campbell except for the described specific bequests to the American Cancer Society, Julie Brown, and Martin Davis. Jean also includes a provision to leave her estate to her son Rodney Campbell if her husband dies before her.

15        IN WITNESS WHEREOF, I hereunto set my hand this _____11_____ day of
_____March_____, 19_89_.

_Jean Campbell_

**(SIGN HERE)**

Signed, sealed, published and declared by the above named Testatrix, as and for her Last Will and Testament, in the presence of us, who at her request, in her presence, and in the presence of one another have hereunto subscribed our names as attesting witnesses, the day and year last written above.

16    _Jerry Gordon_    residing at    _25 State Street_
                                              _Philadelphia, PA_

      _Sharon Gordon_    residing at    _25 State Street_
                                              _Philadelphia, PA_

      _Mark Rogers_    residing at    _25 State Street_
                                              _Philadelphia, PA_

# Glossary

The numbers on this page correspond to the numbers on the model will on the previous page. Important words are defined, and important aspects of the model will are explained.

15. Jean dates and signs the will in front of the witnesses.

16. The Witnesses are the people who after seeing the Testatrix sign and date the will and declare that this is her will, witness the will by signing their names and listing their home addresses at the end of the will. The witnesses must be together and see you sign the will. Most states require only 2 witnesses, but some states require 3 witnesses. Your will form includes 3 signature lines for your protection. The witnesses should be of sound mind, and not be named as beneficiaries in the will.

Affidavit of Subscribing Witnesses

STATE OF _Pennsylvania_ )
                                              ss.:
COUNTY OF _Philadelphia_ )

On _march 11_ , 19_89_ , personally appeared before me, the
undersigned authority

1. _Jean Campbell_          2. _Jerry Gordon_
        Testatrix                      Witness

3. _Sharon Gordon_          4. _Mark Rogers_
        Witness                        Witness

known to me to be the Testatrix and Witnesses, respectively, who being severally sworn state under oath that,
all the subscribing witnesses witnessed the execution of the Will of the within named Testatrix on the same
date they subscribed this instrument; the Testatrix in their presence, subscribed the Will at the end and at the
time of making the subscription declared the instrument to be the Testatrix's Last Will and Testament; at the
request of the Testatrix and in the Testatrix's sight and presence and in the sight and presence of each other,
all the subscribing witnesses witnessed the execution of the Will by the Testatrix by subscribing their names
as witnesses to it; the Testatrix at the time of the execution of the Will, was over the age of 18 years and
appeared to them of sound mind, memory and understanding and was in all respects competent to make a
Will; and the Testator having declared to the said witnesses that she was not under any duress or any undue
influence and that she voluntarily executed this will as her free act and deed.

The subscribing witnesses further state that this affidavit was executed at the request of
the Testatrix, and at the time of the execution of this affidavit the original Will, above described, was exhibited
to them and they identified it as such Will by their signatures appearing on it as subscribing witnesses.

The Testatrix states that each witness was and is competent and of a proper age to witness
a will and further acknowledges that she has read the within instrument and she affirms that each and
every statement made by the subscribing witness is true to her own knowledge.

Severally subscribed,                          TESTATRIX: _Jean Campbell_
acknowledged and sworn to
before me on _march 11, 1989_                  WITNESS: _Jerry Gordon_

                                               WITNESS: _Sharon Gordon_

_mark Davis_                                   WITNESS: _mark Rogers_
Notary Public or Person
Authorized to Take Oaths

# Instructions for Completing the Affidavit of Subscribing Witnesses

An Affidavit of Subscribing Witnesses (also known as a self-proving affidavit), which is recognized in most states, is also included in the will kit. This Affidavit allows you to self-prove your will. A will does not require this affidavit in order for the will to be valid. However, this affidavit may save much time and expense when a will is being probated. A situation in which this might occur is if the witnesses to the will could not be located when the will was being probated. By the will being self-proved, the witnesses will most likely not have to appear in court. A will is self-proved when the Testator (the person who writes the will) and the witnesses to the will, declare that this document is the Testator's will, and that it was properly executed, and sign this affidavit before an officer authorized to administer oaths or a notary public. This affidavit is included in the will and should be used if possible, but again, a will is valid without an affidavit of subscribing witnesses.

If you choose to self-prove your will, use the following instructions:

1. You must sign your will and have it witnessed by three witnesses, and follow the instructions for the execution of a will, as they are given in this book.

2. If there is not an officer authorized to administer oaths or a notary public present at the will signing, you and the witnesses to the will must at a later time, personally appear before such officer or a notary public. All parties must bring proper identification. Advise the officer or notary public that you want to self-prove your will. Ask the officer or notary public if he or she has a form for this purpose. If yes, follow the officer or notary's instructions.

3. If the officer or notary does not have a form, use the Affidavit of Subscribing Witnesses included in this kit.

4. Use the model affidavit of subscribing witnesses as a guide to filling out your affidavit. You and your witnesses should write your names in the spaces designated "Testator" and "witness." The officer or notary will have you swear to the statements made in the affidavit, and to sign your names at the bottom of the affidavit. The officer or notary will date, sign, and place a stamp or seal on the affidavit.

5. At this time, staple the affidavit to the will so that it becomes the last page.

# Last Will and Testament

## of

**2**    _Lewis Finney_

**3**    I, _Lewis Finney_ , presently residing at

**4**    _5 Pheasant Lane, Cleveland, Ohio_ ,

**5**    being of full age and sound and disposing mind and memory, hereby make, publish and declare this to be my Last Will and Testament.

**6**    FIRST: I hereby revoke any and all Wills and Codicils by me anytime heretofore made.

**7**    SECOND: I direct all of my just debts and funeral expenses be paid out of my Estate as soon as practicable after my death.

**8**    THIRD: I hereby nominate and appoint _Ed Warren_ , as Executor/Executrix of this, my Last Will and Testament, and I direct that no bond or other security shall be required of him/her in any jurisdiction. If my said Executor/Executrix hereinabove named is unable to serve as Executor/Executrix then I nominate and appoint

**9**    _Steve Harris_ , Executor/Executrix of this my Last Will and Testament, and I further direct that he/she not be required to post any bond or other security.

**10**    FOURTH: I give to my Executor/Executrix, authority to exercise all the powers, duties, rights and immunities conferred upon fiduciaries by law with full power to sell to mortgage and to lease, and to invest and reinvest all or any part of my Estate on such terms as he/she deems best.

**11**    FIFTH:

_I hereby give devise and bequeath my entire estate to my friend Ed Warren except for the following specific bequests: To my aunt Sylvia Greer, I give $5,000.00. To my friend Steve Harris, I give my 1975 Buick Regal. To my cousin Stanley Davis, I give my entire stamp collection. If Ed Warren shall die before me, then with the exception of the above specific bequests, I leave my entire estate to my friend Steve Harris._

# Glossary

The numbers on this page correspond to the numbers on the model will on the previous page. Important words are defined, and important aspects of the model will are explained.

1. A Last Will & Testament, known simply as a "Will," is a written declaration of how a person intends his property to be disposed of after his death.

2. The Testator is Lewis Finney, the person who is writing the will, and who signs and dates the will.

3. A will must have the full name of the Testator. It is important that the spelling and middle initial, if any, are accurate.

4. A will should also have the Testator's address.

5. The Testator must have the mental capacity to make a will.

6. The will revokes or cancels all former wills and codicils. A codicil is used to add to, remove from, or modify the provisions of a will, and must be signed, declared, and witnessed in the same way as a will.

7. Lewis is including a provision to pay all of his outstanding bills and funeral expenses.

8. The Executor/Executrix is the person that you name in the will to carry out the terms of your will and to administer the estate. The person writing the will (Testator) often will name the beneficiary of the largest portion of the estate as Executor/Executrix. However, the Executor/Executrix is not legally required to be a beneficiary. Your will form provides that the Executor/Executrix not be required to post a bond for the Court.

9. Lewis appoints Ed Warren to settle the affairs of his estate. If Ed is unavailable Lewis appoints Steve Harris.

10. Lewis gives Ed total discretion subject to state law to carry out the terms of the will.

11. Lewis leaves his estate to his friend Ed Warren except for the described specific bequests to Sylvia Greer, Steve Harris, and Stanley Davis. Lewis also includes a provision to leave his estate to his friend Steve Harris if Ed Warren dies before Lewis.

12      IN WITNESS WHEREOF, I hereunto set my hand this _____11_____ day of _____March_____, 19_89_.

_____Lewis Finney_____
(SIGN HERE)

Signed, sealed, published, and declared by the above named Testator, as and for his Last Will and Testament, in the presence of us, who at his request, in his presence, and in the presence of one another have hereunto subscribed our names as attesting witnesses, the day and year last written above.

13    _____Elaine Small_____    residing at    _10 Main Street_
                                                          _Cleveland, Ohio_

    _____David Little_____    residing at    _8 Mill Pond Road_
                                                          _Cleveland, Ohio_

    _____Richard Little_____    residing at    _8 Mill Pond Road_
                                                          _Cleveland, Ohio_

# Glossary

The numbers on this page correspond to the numbers on the model will on the previous page. Important words are defined, and important aspects of the model will are explained.

12. Lewis dates and signs the will in front of the witnesses.

13. The Witnesses are the people who after seeing the Testator sign and date the will and declare that this is his will, witness the will by signing their names and listing their home addresses at the end of the will. The witnesses must be together and see you sign the will. Most states require only 2 witnesses, but some states require 3 witnesses. Your will form includes 3 signature lines for your protection. The witnesses should be of sound mind, and not be named as beneficiaries in the will.

**Affidavit of Subscribing Witnesses**

STATE OF _____Ohio_____ )
                                          ss.:
COUNTY OF _Cuyahoga_ )

On ___March 11___, 19_89_, personally appeared before me, the undersigned authority

1. _Lewis Finney_
   Testator

2. _Elaine Small_
   Witness

3. _David Little_
   Witness

4. _Richard Little_
   Witness

known to me to be the Testator and Witnesses, respectively, who being severally sworn state under oath that, all the subscribing witnesses witnessed the execution of the Will of the within named Testator on the same date they subscribed this instrument; the Testator in their presence, subscribed the Will at the end and at the time of making the subscription declared the instrument to be the Testator's Last Will and Testament; at the request of the Testator and in the Testator's sight and presence and in the sight and presence of each other, all the subscribing witnesses witnessed the execution of the Will by the Testator by subscribing their names as witnesses to it; the Testator at the time of the execution of the Will, was over the age of 18 years and appeared to them of sound mind, memory and understanding and was in all respects competent to make a Will; and the Testator having declared to the said witnesses that he was not under any duress or any undue influence and that he voluntarily executed this will as his free act and deed.

The subscribing witnesses further state that this affidavit was executed at the request of the Testator, and at the time of the execution of this affidavit the original Will, above described, was exhibited to them and they identified it as such Will by their signatures appearing on it as subscribing witnesses.

The Testator states that each witness was and is competent and of a proper age to witness a will and further acknowledges that he has read the within instrument and he affirms that each and every statement made by the subscribing witness is true to his own knowledge.

Severally subscribed,
acknowledged and sworn to
before me on march 11, 1989

_Mark Davis_
Notary Public or Person
Authorized to Take Oaths

TESTATOR: _Lewis Finney_

WITNESS: _Elaine Small_

WITNESS: _David Little_

WITNESS: _Richard Little_

# Instructions for Completing the Affidavit of Subscribing Witnesses

An Affidavit of Subscribing Witnesses (also known as a self-proving affidavit), which is recognized in most states, is also included in the will kit. This Affidavit allows you to self-prove your will. A will does not require this affidavit in order for the will to be valid. However, this affidavit may save much time and expense when a will is being probated. A situation in which this might occur is if the witnesses to the will could not be located when the will was being probated. By the will being self-proved, the witnesses will most likely not have to appear in court. A will is self-proved when the Testator (the person who writes the will) and the witnesses to the will, declare that this document is the Testator's will, and that it was properly executed, and sign this affidavit before an officer authorized to administer oaths or a notary public. This affidavit is included in the will and should be used if possible, but again, a will is valid without an affidavit of subscribing witnesses.

If you choose to self-prove your will, use the following instructions:

1. You must sign your will and have it witnessed by three witnesses, and follow the instructions for the execution of a will, as they are given in this book.

2. If there is not an officer authorized to administer oaths or a notary public present at the will signing, you and the witnesses to the will must at a later time, personally appear before such officer or a notary public. All parties must bring proper identification. Advise the officer or notary public that you want to self-prove your will. Ask the officer or notary public if he or she has a form for this purpose. If yes, follow the officer or notary's instructions.

3. If the officer or notary does not have a form, use the Affidavit of Subscribing Witnesses included in this kit.

4. Use the model affidavit of subscribing witnesses as a guide to filling out your affidavit. You and your witnesses should write your names in the spaces designated "Testator" and "witness." The officer or notary will have you swear to the statements made in the affidavit, and to sign your names at the bottom of the affidavit. The officer or notary will date, sign, and place a stamp or seal on the affidavit.

5. At this time, staple the affidavit to the will so that it becomes the last page.

# BLANK WILL FORMS

# Last Will and Testament

# of

_____

𝕴, _____ ,presently residing at

_____ ,

being of full age and sound and disposing mind and memory, hereby make, publish and declare this to be my Last Will and Testament.

        FIRST: I hereby revoke any and all Wills and Codicils by me anytime heretofore made.

        SECOND: I direct all of my just debts and funeral expenses be paid out of my Estate as soon as practicable after my death.

        THIRD: I am presently married to _____ .

        FOURTH: I hereby give, devise and bequeath all of my Estate, real, personal and mixed, of every kind and nature whatsoever and wheresoever situated, to my beloved husband absolutely and forever.

        FIFTH: In the event that my husband shall predecease me, then and in that event, I give, devise and bequeath my Estate hereinabove mentioned in paragraph "FOURTH" herein, to my beloved child or children or grandchildren surviving me, per stirpes.

        SIXTH: In the event I am not survived by my husband or any children, or grandchildren, then, and in such event, I give, devise and bequeath my said Estate to the following named beneficiary/beneficiaries or their survivor/survivors in equal shares.

a. _____
Name and address of beneficiary

b. _____
Name and address of beneficiary

c. _____
Name and address of beneficiary

d. _____
Name and address of beneficiary

e. _____
Name and address of beneficiary

SEVENTH: I hereby nominate and appoint my beloved husband to be the Executor of this, my Last Will and Testament, and I direct that no bond or other security shall be required of him in any jurisdiction. If my said husband is unable to serve as Executor, then I nominate and appoint _____ Executor/Executrix of this my Last Will and Testament, and I further direct that he/she not be required to post any bond or other security.

EIGHTH: I hereby nominate and appoint my husband as Guardian of the person and property of my minor children. In the event that my husband shall be unable to serve as Guardian, then, and in such event I nominate and appoint _____, Guardian/Co-guardians of the person and property of my minor child or children, and I direct that no bond shall be required of any Guardian herein.

NINTH: I give to my Executor/Executrix, authority to exercise all the powers, duties, rights and immunities conferred upon fiduciaries by law with full power to sell, to mortgage, and to lease, and to invest and re-invest all or any part of my Estate on such terms as he/she deems best.

IN WITNESS WHEREOF, I hereunto set my hand this _____ day of _____, 19 ___.


_____
(SIGN HERE)


Signed, sealed, published and declared by the above named Testatrix, as and for her Last Will and Testament, in the presence of us, who at her request, in her presence, and in the presence of one another have hereunto subscribed our names as attesting witnesses, the day and year last written above.


_____     residing at     _____

_____

_____     residing at     _____

_____

_____     residing at     _____

_____

Your Will is an important legal document. Have a qualified legal professional review it to verify that it is complete and faithful to your wishes, that it will direct your property where you want it to go, and that it will minimize the taxes on your estate. Laws can change; tell your attorney to contact you if laws change in such a way as to materially affect your Will.

# Instructions for #1 Will
# (Married Woman with Minor Children)

Please have these instructions in front of you along with the #1 Will model; it is suggested that you complete the #1 Will using the #1 Will model as your general guide.

1. Your Will should be typed or printed in ink. Do not use a pencil or any other eraseable instrument.

2. Insert your full name, on the line below "LAST WILL AND TESTAMENT OF," and repeat your name and write your address on the next two lines.

3. Write your husband's name in paragraph "THIRD."

4. In paragraph "SIXTH," list the names and addresses of the beneficiary/beneficiaries who are to inherit your estate in equal shares in the event that you are not survived by any husband, children, or grandchildren.

5. In paragraph "SEVENTH," insert the name of the person that you want to serve as Executor/Executrix if your husband does not survive you or is unable for any reason to serve as such.

6. In paragraph "EIGHTH," insert the name of the person or persons who you desire to be guardian or guardians of your minor children, again, in the event that your husband does not survive you or cannot serve for any reason.

7. Get your three witnesses together for the signing of the Will. In front of the three witnesses, date, and sign the Will, at the same time telling the witnesses that this is your Last Will and Testament and that you want them to sign their names as witnesses to your Last Will and Testament. As soon as you are finished dating and signing the Will, then have a witness sign his or her name and place his or her address on the line opposite his or her signature. *NOTE: It is important that no one leaves the room while each person is signing. In other words, each witness will witness your signature and the other witnesses' signatures.*

If you wish to self-prove your Will, pull out the instructions for completing the Affidavit of Subscribing Witnesses.

Affidavit of Subscribing Witnesses

STATE OF _____ )
                                                  ss.:

COUNTY OF _____ )

On _____ , 19___ , personally appeared before me, the undersigned authority

1. _____                 2. _____
        Testatrix                                Witness

3. _____                 4. _____
        Witness                                 Witness

known to me to be the Testatrix and Witnesses, respectively, who being severally sworn state under oath that, all the subscribing witnesses witnessed the execution of the Will of the within named Testatrix on the same date they subscribed this instrument; the Testatrix in their presence, subscribed the Will at the end and at the time of making the subscription declared the instrument to be the Testatrix's Last Will and Testament; at the request of the Testatrix and in the Testatrix's sight and presence and in the sight and presence of each other, all the subscribing witnesses witnessed the execution of the Will by the Testatrix by subscribing their names as witnesses to it; the Testatrix at the time of the execution of the Will, was over the age of 18 years and appeared to them of sound mind, memory and understanding and was in all respects competent to make a Will; and the Testatrix having declared to the said witnesses that she was not under any duress or any undue influence and that she voluntarily executed this will as her free act and deed.

        The subscribing witnesses further state that this affidavit was executed at the request of the Testatrix, and at the time of the execution of this affidavit the original Will, above described, was exhibited to them and they identified it as such Will by their signatures appearing on it as subscribing witnesses.

        The Testatrix states that each witness was and is competent and of a proper age to witness a will and further acknowledges that she has read the within instrument and she affirms that each and every statement made by the subscribing witness is true to her own knowledge.

Severally subscribed,               TESTATRIX: _____
acknowledged and sworn to
before me on _____

                                     WITNESS: _____

                                     WITNESS: _____

_____
Notary Public or Person          WITNESS: _____
Authorized to Take Oaths

# Last Will and Testament

# of

_____

I, _____ , presently residing at

_____ ,

being of full age and sound and disposing mind and memory, hereby make, publish and declare this to be my Last Will and Testament.

        FIRST: I hereby revoke any and all Wills and Codicils by me anytime heretofore made.

        SECOND: I direct all of my just debts and funeral expenses be paid out of my Estate as soon as practicable after my death.

        THIRD: I am presently married to _____ .

        FOURTH: I hereby give, devise and bequeath all of my Estate, real, personal and mixed, of every kind and nature whatsoever and wheresoever situated, to my beloved wife absolutely and forever.

        FIFTH: In the event that my wife shall predecease me, then and in that event, I give, devise and bequeath my Estate hereinabove mentioned in paragraph "FOURTH" herein, to my beloved child or children or grandchildren surviving me, per stirpes.

        SIXTH: In the event I am not survived by my wife or any children, or grandchildren, then, and in such event, I give, devise and bequeath my said Estate to the following named beneficiary/beneficiaries or their survivor/survivors in equal shares.

a. _____
Name and address of beneficiary

b. _____
Name and address of beneficiary

c. _____
Name and address of beneficiary

d. _____
Name and address of beneficiary

e. _____
Name and address of beneficiary

SEVENTH: I hereby nominate and appoint my beloved wife to be the Executrix of this, my Last Will and Testament, and I direct that no bond or other security shall be required of her in any jurisdiction. If my said wife is unable to serve as Executrix, then I nominate and appoint _____, Executor/Executrix of this my Last Will and Testament, and I further direct that he/she not be required to post any bond or other security.

EIGHTH: I hereby nominate and appoint my wife as Guardian of the person and property of my minor children. In the event that my wife shall be unable to serve as Guardian, then, and in such event I nominate and appoint _____ Guardian/Co-guardians of the person and property of my minor child or children, and I direct that no bond shall be required of any Guardian herein.

NINTH: I give to my Executor/Executrix, authority to exercise all the powers, duties, rights and immunities conferred upon fiduciaries by law with full power to sell, to mortgage, and to lease, and to invest and reinvest all or any part of my Estate on such terms as he/she deems best.

IN WITNESS WHEREOF, I hereunto set my hand this _____day of _____, 19 ___.

_____
(SIGN HERE)

Signed, sealed, published and declared by the above named Testator, as and for his Last Will and Testament, in the presence of us, who at his request, in his presence, and in the presence of one another have hereunto subscribed our names as attesting witnesses, the day and year last written above.

_____    residing at    _____

                                           _____

_____    residing at    _____

                                           _____

_____    residing at    _____

                                           _____

Your Will is an important legal document. Have a qualified legal professional review it to verify that it is complete and faithful to your wishes, that it will direct your property where you want it to go, and that it will minimize the taxes on your estate. Laws can change; tell your attorney to contact you if laws change in such a way as to materially affect your Will.

# Instructions for #2 Will
# (Married Man with Minor Children)

Please have these instructions in front of you along with the #2 Will model. It is suggested that you complete the #2 Will using the #2 Will model as your general guide.

1. Your Will should be typed or printed in ink. Do not use a pencil or any other eraseable instrument.

2. Insert your full name, on the line below "LAST WILL AND TESTAMENT OF," and repeat your name and write your address on the next two lines.

3. Write your wife's name in paragraph "THIRD."

4. In paragraph "SIXTH," list the names, and addresses of the beneficiary/beneficiaries who are to inherit your estate in equal shares in the event that you are not survived by any wife, children, or grandchildren.

5. In paragraph "SEVENTH," insert the name of the person that you want to serve as Executor/Executrix if your wife does not survive you or is unable for any reason to serve as such.

6. In paragraph "EIGHTH," insert the name of the person or persons who you desire to be guardian or guardians of your minor children, again, in the event that your wife does not survive you or cannot serve for any reason.

7. Get your three witnesses together for the signing of the Will. In front of the three witnesses, date, and sign the Will, at the same time telling the witnesses that this is your Last Will and Testament and that you want them to sign their names as witnesses to your Last Will and Testament. As soon as you are finished dating and signing the Will, then have witness sign his or her name and place his or her address on the line opposite his or her signature. *NOTE: It is important that no one leaves the room while each person is signing. In other words, each witness will witness your signature and the other witnesses' signatures.*

If you wish to self-prove your Will, pull out the instructions for completing the Affidavit of Subscribing Witnesses.

**Affidavit of Subscribing Witnesses**

STATE OF _____)

ss.:

COUNTY OF _____)

On _____ , 19___ , personally appeared before me, the undersigned authority

1. _____     2. _____
       Testator                                        Witness

3. _____     4. _____
       Witness                                        Witness

known to me to be the Testator and Witnesses, respectively, who being severally sworn state under oath that, all the subscribing witnesses witnessed the execution of the Will of the within named Testator on the same date they subscribed this instrument; the Testator in their presence, subscribed the Will at the end and at the time of making the subscription declared the instrument to be the Testator's Last Will and Testament; at the request of the Testator and in the Testator's sight and presence and in the sight and presence of each other, all the subscribing witnesses witnessed the execution of the Will by the Testator by subscribing their names as witnesses to it; the Testator at the time of the execution of the Will, was over the age of 18 years and appeared to them of sound mind, memory and understanding and was in all respects competent to make a Will; and the Testator having declared to the said witnesses that he was not under any duress or any undue influence and that he voluntarily executed this will as his free act and deed.

The subscribing witnesses further state that this affidavit was executed at the request of the Testator, and at the time of the execution of this affidavit the original Will, above described, was exhibited to them and they identified it as such Will by their signatures appearing on it as subscribing witnesses.

The Testator states that each witness was and is competent and of a proper age to witness a will and further acknowledges that he has read the within instrument and he affirms that each and every statement made by the subscribing witness is true to his own knowledge.

Severally subscribed,          TESTATOR: _____
acknowledged and sworn to
before me on _____       WITNESS: _____

                                        WITNESS: _____

_____
Notary Public or Person
Authorized to Take Oaths          WITNESS: _____

# Last Will and Testament

## of

_____

I, _____ , presently residing at
_____ ,
being of full age and sound and disposing mind and memory, hereby make, publish and declare this to be
my Last Will and Testament.

FIRST: I hereby revoke any and all Wills and Codicils by me anytime heretofore made.

SECOND: I direct all of my just debts and funeral expenses be paid out of my Estate as
soon as practicable after my death.

THIRD: I am presently married to _____ .

FOURTH: I hereby give, devise and bequeath all of my Estate, real, personal and mixed, of
every kind and nature whatsoever and wheresoever situated, to my beloved husband absolutely and forever.

FIFTH: In the event that my husband shall predecease me, then and in that event, I give,
devise and bequeath my Estate hereinabove mentioned in paragraph "FOURTH" herein, to my beloved
child or children or grandchildren surviving me, per stirpes.

SIXTH: In the event I am not survived by my husband or any children, or grandchildren,
then, and in such event, I give, devise and bequeath my said Estate to the following named
beneficiary/beneficiaries or their survivor/survivors in equal shares.

a. _____
Name and address of beneficiary

b. _____
Name and address of beneficiary

c. _____
Name and address of beneficiary

d. _____
Name and address of beneficiary

e. _____
Name and address of beneficiary

SEVENTH: I hereby nominate and appoint my beloved husband to be the Executor of this, my Last Will and Testament, and I direct that no bond or other security shall be required of him in any jurisdiction. If my said husband is unable to serve as Executor, then I nominate and appoint _____, Executor/Executrix of this my Last Will and Testament, and I further direct that he/she not be required to post any bond or other security.

EIGHTH: I give to my Executor/Executrix, authority to exercise all the powers, duties, rights and immunities conferred upon fiduciaries by law with full power to sell to mortgage and to lease, and to invest and reinvest all or any part of my Estate on such terms as he/she deems best.

IN WITNESS WHEREOF, I hereunto set my hand this _____ day of _____, 19 ___.

_____
(SIGN HERE)


Signed, sealed, published and declared by the above named Testatrix, as and for her Last Will and Testament, in the presence of us, who at her request, in her presence, and in the presence of one another have hereunto subscribed our names as attesting witnesses, the day and year last written above.

_____  residing at  _____

                                                      _____

_____  residing at  _____

                                                      _____

_____  residing at  _____

                                                      _____

Your Will is an important legal document. Have a qualified legal professional review it to verify that it is complete and faithful to your wishes, that it will direct your property where you want it to go, and that it will minimize the taxes on your estate. Laws can change; tell your attorney to contact you if laws change in such a way as to materially affect your Will.

# Instructions for #3 Will
# (Married Woman without Minor Children)

Please have these instructions in front of you along with the #3 Will model. It is suggested that you complete the #3 Will using the #3 Will model as your general guide.

1. Your Will should be typed or printed in ink. Do not use a pencil or any other eraseable instrument.

2. Insert your full name, on the line below "LAST WILL AND TESTAMENT OF," and repeat your name and write your address on the next two lines.

3. Write your husband's name in paragraph "THIRD."

4. In paragraph "SIXTH," list the names and addresses of the beneficiary/beneficiaries who are to inherit your estate in equal shares in the event that you are not survived by any husband, children, or grandchildren.

5. In paragraph "SEVENTH," insert the name of the person that you want to serve as Executor/Executrix if your husband does not survive you or is unable for any reason to serve as such.

6. Get your three witnesses together for the signing of the Will. In front of the three witnesses, date, and sign the Will, at the same time telling the witnesses that this is your Last Will and Testament and that you want them to sign their names as witnesses to your Last Will and Testament. As soon as you are finished dating and signing the Will, have a witness sign his or her name and place his or her address on the line opposite his or her signature. *NOTE: It is important that no one leaves the room while each person is signing. In other words, each witness will witness your signature and the other witnesses' signatures.*

If you wish to self-prove your Will, pull out the instructions for completing the Affidavit of Subscribing Witnesses.

Affidavit of Subscribing Witnesses

STATE OF _____)

                                    ss.:

COUNTY OF _____)

On _____, 19___, personally appeared before me, the undersigned authority

1. _____        2. _____

       Testatrix                            Witness

3. _____        4. _____

       Witness                            Witness

known to me to be the Testatrix and Witnesses, respectively, who being severally sworn state under oath that, all the subscribing witnesses witnessed the execution of the Will of the within named Testatrix on the same date they subscribed this instrument; the Testatrix in their presence, subscribed the Will at the end and at the time of making the subscription declared the instrument to be the Testatrix's Last Will and Testament; at the request of the Testatrix and in the Testatrix's sight and presence and in the sight and presence of each other, all the subscribing witnesses witnessed the execution of the Will by the Testatrix by subscribing their names as witnesses to it; the Testatrix at the time of the execution of the Will, was over the age of 18 years and appeared to them of sound mind, memory and understanding and was in all respects competent to make a Will; and the Testatrix having declared to the said witnesses that she was not under any duress or any undue influence and that she voluntarily executed this will as her free act and deed.

The subscribing witnesses further state that this affidavit was executed at the request of the Testatrix, and at the time of the execution of this affidavit the original Will, above described, was exhibited to them and they identified it as such Will by their signatures appearing on it as subscribing witnesses.

The Testatrix states that each witness was and is competent and of a proper age to witness a will and further acknowledges that she has read the within instrument and she affirms that each and every statement made by the subscribing witness is true to her own knowledge.

Severally subscribed,            TESTATRIX: _____
acknowledged and sworn to
before me on _____      WITNESS:   _____

                                       WITNESS:   _____

_____      WITNESS:   _____
Notary Public or Person
Authorized to Take Oaths

# Last Will and Testament

# of

_____

**I,** _____ , presently residing at

_____ ,

being of full age and sound and disposing mind and memory, hereby make, publish and declare this to be my Last Will and Testament.

       FIRST: I hereby revoke any and all Wills and Codicils by me anytime heretofore made.

       SECOND: I direct all of my just debts and funeral expenses be paid out of my Estate as soon as practicable after my death.

       THIRD: I am presently married to _____ .

       FOURTH: I hereby give, devise and bequeath all of my Estate, real, personal and mixed, of every kind and nature whatsoever and wheresoever situated, to my beloved wife absolutely and forever.

       FIFTH: In the event that my wife shall predecease me, then and in that event, I give, devise and bequeath my Estate hereinabove mentioned in paragraph "FOURTH" herein, to my beloved child or children or grandchildren surviving me, per stirpes.

       SIXTH: In the event I am not survived by my wife or any children, or grandchildren, then, and in such event, I give, devise and bequeath my said Estate to the following named beneficiary/beneficiaries or their survivor/survivors in equal shares.

a. _____
Name and address of beneficiary

b. _____
Name and address of beneficiary

c. _____
Name and address of beneficiary

d. _____
Name and address of beneficiary

e. _____
Name and address of beneficiary

SEVENTH: I hereby nominate and appoint my beloved wife to be the Executrix of this, my Last Will and Testament, and I direct that no bond or other security shall be required of her in any jurisdiction. If my said wife is unable to serve as Executrix, then I nominate and appoint _____, Executor/Executrix of this my Last Will and Testament, and I further direct that he/she not be required to post any bond or other security.

EIGHTH: I give to my Executor/Executrix, authority to exercise all the powers, duties, rights and immunities conferred upon fiduciaries by law with full power to sell to mortgage and to lease, and to invest and re-invest all or any part of my Estate on such terms as he/she deems best.

IN WITNESS WHEREOF, I hereunto set my hand this _____ day of _____, 19 ___.

_____
(SIGN HERE)

Signed, sealed, published and declared by the above named Testator, as and for his Last Will and Testament, in the presence of us, who at his request, in his presence, and in the presence of one another have hereunto subscribed our names as attesting witnesses, the day and year last written above.

_____ residing at _____

_____

_____ residing at _____

_____

_____ residing at _____

_____

Your Will is an important legal document. Have a qualified legal professional review it to verify that it is complete and faithful to your wishes, that it will direct your property where you want it to go, and that it will minimize the taxes on your estate. Laws can change; tell your attorney to contact you if laws change in such a way as to materially affect your Will.

# Instructions for #4 Will
# (Married Man without Minor Children)

Please have these instructions in front of you along with the #4 Will model. It is suggested that you complete the #4 Will using the #4 Will model as your general guide.

1.  Your Will should be typed or printed in ink. Do not use a pencil or any other eraseable instrument.

2.  Insert your full name, on the line below "LAST WILL AND TESTAMENT OF," and repeat your name and write your address on the next two lines.

3.  Write your wife's name in paragraph "THIRD."

4.  In paragraph "SIXTH," list the names, and addresses of the beneficiary/beneficiaries who are to inherit your estate in equal shares in the event that you are not survived by any wife, children, or grandchildren.

5.  In paragraph "SEVENTH," insert the name of the person that you want to serve as Executor/Executrix if your wife does not survive you or is unable for any reason to serve as such.

6.  Get your three witnesses together for the signing of the Will. In front of the three witnesses, date, and sign the Will, at the same time telling the witnesses that this is your Last Will and Testament and that you want them to sign their names as witnesses to your Last Will and Testament. As soon as you are finished dating and signing the Will, have a witness sign his or her name and place his or her address on the line opposite his or her signature. *NOTE: It is important that no one leaves the room while each person is signing. In other words, each witness will witness your signature and the other witnesses' signatures.*

If you wish to self-prove your Will, pull out the instructions for completing the Affidavit of Subscribing Witnesses.

Affidavit of Subscribing Witnesses

STATE OF _____)
                                         ss.:

COUNTY OF _____)

On _____ , 19___ , personally appeared before me, the undersigned
authority

1. _____    2. _____
          Testator                                   Witness

3. _____    4. _____
          Witness                                  Witness

known to me to be the Testator and Witnesses, respectively, who being severally sworn state under oath
that, all the subscribing witnesses witnessed the execution of the Will of the within named Testator on the
same date they subscribed this instrument; the Testator in their presence, subscribed the Will at the end
and at the time of making the subscription declared the instrument to be the Testator's Last Will and
Testament; at the request of the Testator and in the Testator's sight and presence and in the sight and
presence of each other, all the subscribing witnesses witnessed the execution of the Will by the Testator by
subscribing their names as witnesses to it; the Testator at the time of the execution of the Will, was over
the age of 18 years and appeared to them of sound mind, memory and understanding and was in all
respects competent to make a Will; and the Testator having declared to the said witnesses that he was not
under any duress or any undue influence and that he voluntarily executed this will as his free act and deed.

      The subscribing witnesses further state that this affidavit was executed at the request of the
Testator, and at the time of the execution of this affidavit the original Will, above described, was exhibited
to them and they identified it as such Will by their signatures appearing on it as subscribing witnesses.

      The Testator states that each witness was and is competent and of a proper age to witness a
will and further acknowledges that he has read the within instrument and he affirms that each and every
statement made by the subscribing witness is true to his own knowledge.

Severally subscribed,         TESTATOR: _____
acknowledged and sworn to
before me on _____      WITNESS: _____

                                   WITNESS: _____
_____
Notary Public or Person
Authorized to Take Oaths        WITNESS: _____

# Last Will and Testament

# of

_____

I, _____ , presently residing at

_____ ,

being of full age and sound and disposing mind and memory, hereby make, publish and declare this to be

my Last Will and Testament.

        FIRST: I hereby revoke any and all Wills and Codicils by me anytime heretofore made.

        SECOND: I direct all of my just debts and funeral expenses be paid out of my Estate as

soon as practicable after my death.

        THIRD:        a. I am presently not married.

                    b. I am the parent of the following child/children:

1. _____    2. _____

3. _____    4. _____

5. _____    6. _____

        FOURTH: I hereby give, devise and bequeath all of my Estate, real, personal and mixed,

of every kind and nature whatsoever and wheresoever situated, to my beloved child or children or

grandchildren surviving me, per stirpes.

        FIFTH: I nominate and appoint _____ , as

Executor/Executrix of this Will. In the event he/she shall predecease me or fails to serve as such

Executor/Executrix, then in such event, I nominate and appoint _____ ,

Executor/Executrix of this my Last Will and Testament. I further direct that no appointee hereunder shall

be required to give any bond for the faithful performance of his/her duties.

        SIXTH: In the event that any child/children of mine shall be minors at my death and shall

not be survived by their natural parent, I then nominate and appoint _____ as

Guardian of the person and property of my minor child/children. In the event that

_____ shall be unable or unwilling to serve as Guardian, then, and in

such event I nominate and appoint _____ Guardian of the person and

property of my minor child or children, and I direct that no bond shall be required of any Guardian herein.

SEVENTH: I give to my Executor/Executrix, the authority to exercise all the powers, duties, rights and immunities conferred upon fiduciaries by law with full power to sell to mortgage and to lease, and to invest and reinvest all or any part of my Estate on such terms as he/she deems best.

IN WITNESS WHEREOF, I hereunto set my hand this _____ day of _____, 19___ .

_____

(SIGN HERE)

Signed, sealed, published and declared by the above named Testator/Testatrix, as and for his/her Last Will and Testament, in the presence of us, who at his/her request, in his/her presence, and in the presence of one another have hereunto subscribed our names as attesting witnesses, the day and year last written above.

_____     residing at     _____

_____

_____     residing at     _____

_____

_____     residing at     _____

_____

Your Will is an important legal document. Have a qualified legal professional review it to verify that it is complete and faithful to your wishes, that it will direct your property where you want it to go, and that it will minimize the taxes on your estate. Laws can change; tell your attorney to contact you if laws change in such a way as to materially affect your Will.

# Instructions for #5 Will
# (Unmarried Individual with Minor Children)

Please have these instructions in front of you along with the #5 Will model. It is suggested that you complete the #5 Will using the #5 Will model as your general guide.

1.  Your Will should be typed or printed in ink. Do not use a pencil or any other eraseable instrument.

2.  Insert your full name, on the line below "LAST WILL AND TESTAMENT OF," and repeat your name and write your address on the next two lines.

3.  Write your child or children's name(s) in paragraph "THIRD."

4.  In paragraph "FIFTH," insert the name of the person that you want to serve as Executor/Executrix, and if that person does not survive you or is unable to serve for any reason, insert the name of an alternate Executor/Executrix.

5.  In paragraph "SIXTH," insert the name of the person who you desire to be guardian of your minor child/children, in the event that their natural parent does not survive you, or is unable to serve for any reason. Then insert the name of an alternate guardian in the event that the above person does not survive you or is unable to serve for any reason.

6.  Get your three witnesses together for the signing of the Will. In front of the three witnesses, date and sign the Will, at the same time telling the witnesses that this is your Last Will and Testament and that you want them to sign their names as witnesses to your Last Will and Testament. As soon as you are finished dating and signing the Will, have a witness sign his or her name and place his or her address on the line opposite his or her signature. *NOTE: It is important that no one leaves the room while each person is signing. In other words, each witness will witness your signature and the other witnesses' signatures.*

If you wish to self-prove your will, pull out the instructions for completing the Affidavit of Subscribing Witnesses.

## Affidavit of Subscribing Witnesses

STATE OF _____)

                                     ss.:

COUNTY OF _____)

On _____ , 19___ , personally appeared before me, the undersigned authority

1. _____    2. _____
       Testator/Testatrix                           Witness

3. _____    4. _____
       Witness                                  Witness

known to me to be the Testator/Testatrix and Witnesses, respectively, who being severally sworn state under oath that, all the subscribing witnesses witnessed the execution of the Will of the within named Testator/Testatrix on the same date they subscribed this instrument; the Testator/Testatrix in their presence, subscribed the Will at the end and at the time of making the subscription declared the instrument to be the Testator/Testatrix's Last Will and Testament; at the request of the Testator/Testatrix and in the Testator/Testatrix's sight and presence and in the sight and presence of each other, all the subscribing witnesses witnessed the execution of the Will by the Testator/Testatrix by subscribing their names as witnesses to it; the Testator/Testatrix at the time of the execution of the Will, was over the age of 18 years and appeared to them of sound mind, memory and understanding and was in all respects competent to make a Will; and the Testator/Testatrix having declared to the said witnesses that he was not under any duress or any undue influence and that he voluntarily executed this will as his/her free act and deed.

      The subscribing witnesses further state that this affidavit was executed at the request of the Testator/Testatrix, and at the time of the execution of this affidavit the original Will, above described, was exhibited to them and they identified it as such Will by their signatures appearing on it as subscribing witnesses.

      The Testator/Testatrix states that each witness was and is competent and of a proper age to witness a will and further acknowledges that he/she has read the within instrument and he/she affirms that each and every statement made by the subscribing witness is true to his/her own knowledge.

Severally subscribed,      TESTATOR/TESTATRIX: _____
acknowledged and sworn to
before me on _____      WITNESS: _____

                      WITNESS: _____
_____
Notary Public or Person
Authorized to Take Oaths      WITNESS: _____

# Last Will and Testament

# of

_____

I, _____ , presently residing at

_____ ,

being of full age and sound and disposing mind and memory, hereby make, publish and declare this to be

my Last Will and Testament.

FIRST: I hereby revoke any and all Wills and Codicils by me anytime heretofore made.

SECOND: I direct all of my just debts and funeral expenses be paid out of my Estate as

soon as practicable after my death.

THIRD:　　a. I am presently not married.

b. I am the parent of the following child/children:

1. _____　2. _____

3. _____　4. _____

5. _____　6. _____

FOURTH: I hereby give, devise and bequeath all of my Estate, real, personal and mixed,

of every kind and nature whatsoever and wheresoever situated, to my beloved child or children or

grandchildren surviving me, per stirpes.

FIFTH: I nominate and appoint _____ , as

Executor/Executrix of this Will. In the event he/she shall predecease me or fails to serve as such

Executor/Executrix, then in such event, I nominate and appoint _____ ,

Executor/Executrix of this my Last Will and Testament. I further direct that no appointee hereunder shall

be required to give any bond for the faithful performance of his/her duties.

SIXTH: I give to my Executor/Executrix, the authority to exercise all the powers, duties,

rights and immunities conferred upon fiduciaries by law with full power to sell to mortgage and to lease,

and to invest and reinvest all or any part of my Estate on such terms as he/she deems best.

IN WITNESS WHEREOF, I hereunto set my hand this _____ day of _____, 19____ .

_____

(SIGN HERE)

Signed, sealed, published and declared by the above named Testatrix, as and for his/her Last Will and Testament, in the presence of us, who at his/her request, in his/her presence, and in the presence of one another have hereunto subscribed our names as attesting witnesses, the day and year last written above.

_____    residing at    _____
                                          _____

_____    residing at    _____
                                          _____

_____    residing at    _____
                                          _____

Your Will is an important legal document. Have a qualified legal professional review it to verify that it is complete and faithful to your wishes, that it will direct your property where you want it to go, and that it will minimize the taxes on your estate. Laws can change; tell your attorney to contact you if laws change in such a way as to materially affect your Will.

# Instructions for #6 Will
# (Unmarried Individual with Adult Children)

Please have these instructions in front of you along with the #6 Will model. It is suggested that you complete the #6 Will using the #6 Will model as your general guide.

1.  Your Will should be typed or printed in ink. Do not use a pencil or any other eraseable instrument.

2.  Insert your full name, on the line below "LAST WILL AND TESTAMENT OF," and repeat your name and write your address on the next two lines.

3.  Write your child or children's name(s) in paragraph "THIRD."

4.  In paragraph "FIFTH," insert the name of the person that you want to serve as Executor/Executrix, and if that person does not survive you or is unable to serve for any reason, insert the name of an alternate Executor/Executrix.

5.  Get your three witnesses together for the signing of the Will. In front of the three witnesses, date and sign the Will, at the same time telling the witnesses that this is your Last Will and Testament and that you want them to sign their names as witnesses to your Last Will and Testament. As soon as you are finished dating and signing the Will, have a witness sign his or her name and place his or her address on the line opposite his or her signature. *NOTE: It is important that no one leaves the room while each person is signing. In other words, each witness will witness your signature and the other witnesses' signatures.*

If you wish to self-prove your will, pull out the instructions for completing the Affidavit of Subscribing Witnesses.

Affidavit of Subscribing Witnesses

STATE OF    _____)

                                            ss.:

COUNTY OF _____)

          On _____ , 19\_\_\_ , personally appeared before me, the undersigned authority

1. _____        2. _____
            Testator/Testatrix                             Witness

3. _____        4. _____
                Witness                             Witness

known to me to be the Testator/Testatrix and Witnesses, respectively, who being severally sworn state under oath that, all the subscribing witnesses witnessed the execution of the Will of the within named Testator/Testatrix on the same date they subscribed this instrument; the Testator/Testatrix in their presence, subscribed the Will at the end and at the time of making the subscription declared the instrument to be the Testator/Testatrix's Last Will and Testament; at the request of the Testator/Testatrix and in the Testator/Testatrix's sight and presence and in the sight and presence of each other, all the subscribing witnesses witnessed the execution of the Will by the Testator/Testatrix by subscribing their names as witnesses to it; the Testator/Testatrix at the time of the execution of the Will, was over the age of 18 years and appeared to them of sound mind, memory and understanding and was in all respects competent to make a Will; and the Testator/Testatrix having declared to the said witnesses that he/she was not under any duress or any undue influence and that he/she voluntarily executed this will as his/her free act and deed.

      The subscribing witnesses further state that this affidavit was executed at the request of the Testator/Testatrix, and at the time of the execution of this affidavit the original Will, above described, was exhibited to them and they identified it as such Will by their signatures appearing on it as subscribing witnesses.

      The Testator/Testatrix states that each witness was and is competent and of a proper age to witness a will and further acknowledges that he/she has read the within instrument and he/she affirms that each and every statement made by the subscribing witness is true to his/her own knowledge.

Severally subscribed,          TESTATOR/TESTATRIX:   _____
acknowledged and sworn to
before me on _____         WITNESS:   _____

                               WITNESS:   _____
_____
Notary Public or Person
Authorized to Take Oaths           WITNESS:   _____

# Last Will and Testament

# of

_____

$\mathfrak{I}$, _____ , presently residing at

_____ ,

being of full age and sound and disposing mind and memory, hereby make, publish and declare this to be my Last Will and Testament.

FIRST: I hereby revoke any and all Wills and Codicils by me anytime heretofore made.

SECOND: I direct all of my just debts and funeral expenses be paid out of my Estate as soon as practicable after my death.

THIRD:  I am presently not married.

FOURTH: I hereby give, devise and bequeath all of my Estate, real, personal and mixed, of every kind and nature whatsoever and wheresoever situated, to _____.

FIFTH: In the event that I am not survived by _____ , I give, devise and bequeath my said estate to _____.

SIXTH: I nominate and appoint , as Executor/Executrix of this Will. In the event he/she shall predecease me or fails to serve as such Executor/Executrix, then in such event, I nominate and appoint _____ , Executor/Executrix of this my Last Will and Testament. I further direct that no appointee hereunder shall be required to give any bond for the faithful performance of his/her duties.

SEVENTH: I give to my Executor/Executrix, authority to exercise all the powers, duties, rights and immunities conferred upon fiduciaries by law with full power to sell to mortgage and to lease, and to invest and reinvest all or any part of my Estate on such terms as he/she deems best.

IN WITNESS WHEREOF, I hereunto set my hand this _____ day of
_____, 19___ .

_____
(SIGN HERE)

Signed, sealed, published and declared by the above named Testator/Testatrix, as and for his/her Last Will and Testament, in the presence of us, who at his/her request, in his/her presence, and in the presence of one another have hereunto subscribed our names as attesting witnesses, the day and year last written above.

_____    residing at    _____
                                           _____

_____    residing at    _____
                                           _____

_____    residing at    _____
                                           _____

Your Will is an important legal document. Have a qualified legal professional review it to verify that it is complete and faithful to your wishes, that it will direct your property where you want it to go, and that it will minimize the taxes on your estate. Laws can change; tell your attorney to contact you if laws change in such a way as to materially affect your Will.

# Instructions for #7 Will
# (Unmarried Individual with No Children & One Beneficiary)

Please have these instructions in front of you along with the #7 Will model. It is suggested that you complete the #7 Will using the #7 Will model as your general guide.

1.   Your Will should be typed or printed in ink. Do not use a pencil or any other eraseable instrument.

2.   Insert your full name, on the line below "LAST WILL AND TESTAMENT OF," and repeat your name and write your address on the next two lines.

3.   In paragraph "FOURTH," insert the name of the beneficiary who is to inherit your estate.

4.   In paragraph "FIFTH," insert the name of the beneficiary who is to inherit your estate if the beneficiary named in paragraph "FOURTH" does not survive you.

5.   In paragraph "SIXTH," insert the name of the person that you want to serve as Executor/Executrix, and if that person does not survive you or is unable to serve for any reason, insert the name of an alternate Executor/Executrix.

6.   Get your three witnesses together for the signing of the Will. In front of the three witnesses, date and sign the Will, at the same time telling the witnesses that this is your Last Will and Testament and that you want them to sign their names as witnesses to your Last Will and Testament. As soon as you are finished dating and signing the Will, have a witness sign his or her name and place his or her address on the line opposite his or her signature. *NOTE: It is important that no one leaves the room while each person is signing. In other words, each witness will witness your signature and the other witnesses' signatures.*

If you wish to self-prove your will, pull out the instructions for completing the Affidavit of Subscribing Witnesses.

Affidavit of Subscribing Witnesses

STATE OF _____)

                                             ss.:

COUNTY OF _____)

On _____ , 19___ , personally appeared before me, the undersigned authority

1. _____

          Testator/Testatrix

2. _____

          Witness

3. _____

          Witness

4. _____

          Witness

known to me to be the Testator/Testatrix and Witnesses, respectively, who being severally sworn state under oath that, all the subscribing witnesses witnessed the execution of the Will of the within named Testator/Testatrix on the same date they subscribed this instrument; the Testator/Testatrix in their presence, subscribed the Will at the end and at the time of making the subscription declared the instrument to be the Testator/Testatrix's Last Will and Testament; at the request of the Testator/Testatrix and in the Testator/Testatrix's sight and presence and in the sight and presence of each other, all the subscribing witnesses witnessed the execution of the Will by the Testator/Testatrix by subscribing their names as witnesses to it; the Testator/Testatrix at the time of the execution of the Will, was over the age of 18 years and appeared to them of sound mind, memory and understanding and was in all respects competent to make a Will; and the Testator/Testatrix having declared to the said witnesses that he/she was not under any duress or any undue influence and that he/she voluntarily executed this will as his/her free act and deed.

       The subscribing witnesses further state that this affidavit was executed at the request of the Testator/Testatrix, and at the time of the execution of this affidavit the original Will, above described, was exhibited to them and they identified it as such Will by their signatures appearing on it as subscribing witnesses.

       The Testator/Testatrix states that each witness was and is competent and of a proper age to witness a will and further acknowledges that he/she has read the within instrument and he/she affirms that each and every statement made by the subscribing witness is true to his/her own knowledge.

Severally subscribed,
acknowledged and sworn to
before me on _____

_____
Notary Public or Person
Authorized to Take Oaths

TESTATOR/TESTATRIX: _____

WITNESS: _____

WITNESS: _____

WITNESS: _____

# Last Will and Testament

## of

_____

**I,** _____ , presently residing at

_____

being of full age and sound and disposing mind and memory, hereby make, publish and declare this to be my Last Will and Testament.

 FIRST: I hereby revoke any and all Wills and Codicils by me anytime heretofore made.

 SECOND: I direct all of my just debts and funeral expenses be paid out of my Estate as soon as practicable after my death.

 THIRD: I am presently not married.

 FOURTH: I hereby give, devise and bequeath all of my Estate, real, personal and mixed, of every kind and nature whatsoever and wheresoever situated, to the following named beneficiaries or their survivors in equal shares.


a. _____
Name and address of beneficiary

b. _____
Name and address of beneficiary

c. _____
Name and address of beneficiary

d. _____
Name and address of beneficiary

e. _____
Name and address of beneficiary

 FIFTH: I nominate and appoint _____ ,
as Executor/Executrix of this Will. In the event he/she shall predecease me or fails to serve as such Executor/Executrix, then in such event, I nominate and appoint _____ ,
Executor/Executrix of this my Last Will and Testament. I further direct that no appointee hereunder shall be required to give any bond for the faithful performance of his/her duties.

SIXTH: I give to my Executor/Executrix, authority to exercise all the powers, duties, rights and immunities conferred upon fiduciaries by law with full power to sell to mortgage and to lease, and to invest and reinvest all or any part of my Estate on such terms as he/she deems best.

IN WITNESS WHEREOF, I hereunto set my hand this _____ day of _____, 19___ .

_____
(SIGN HERE)

Signed, sealed, published and declared by the above named Testator/Testatrix, as and for his/her Last Will and Testament, in the presence of us, who at his/her request, in his/her presence, and in the presence of one another have hereunto subscribed our names as attesting witnesses, the day and year last written above.

_____ residing at _____

_____

_____ residing at _____

_____

_____ residing at _____

_____

Your Will is an important legal document. Have a qualified legal professional review it to verify that it is complete and faithful to your wishes, that it will direct your property where you want it to go, and that it will minimize the taxes on your estate. Laws can change; tell your attorney to contact you if laws change in such a way as to materially affect your Will.

# Instructions for #8 Will
# (Unmarried Individual with No Children and Two or More Beneficiaries)

Please have these instructions in front of you along with the #8 Will model. It is suggested that you complete the #8 Will using the #8 Will model as your general guide.

1.  Your Will should be typed or printed in ink. Do not use a pencil or any other eraseable instrument.

2.  Insert your full name, on the line below "LAST WILL AND TESTAMENT OF," and repeat your name and write your address on the next two lines.

3.  In paragraph "FOURTH," insert the name of the beneficiaries who are to inherit your estate.

4.  In paragraph "FIFTH," insert the name of the person that you want to serve as Executor/Executrix, and if that person does not survive you or is unable to serve for any reason, insert the name of an alternate Executor/Executrix.

5.  Get your three witnesses together for the signing of the Will. In front of the three witnesses, date and sign the Will, at the same time telling the witnesses that this is your Last Will and Testament and that you want them to sign their names as witnesses to your Last Will and Testament. As soon as you are finished dating and signing the Will, have a witness sign his or her name and place his or her address on the line opposite his or her signature. *NOTE: It is important that no one leaves the room while each person is signing. In other words, each witness will witness your signature and the other witnesses' signatures.*

If you wish to self-prove your will, pull out the instructions for completing the Affidavit of Subscribing Witnesses.

**Affidavit of Subscribing Witnesses**

STATE OF _____)

                                        ss.:

COUNTY OF _____)

On _____ , 19___ , personally appeared before me, the undersigned authority

1. _____     2. _____
          Testator/Testatrix                                  Witness

3. _____     4. _____
               Witness                                    Witness

known to me to be the Testator/Testatrix and Witnesses, respectively, who being severally sworn state under oath that, all the subscribing witnesses witnessed the execution of the Will of the within named Testator/Testatrix on the same date they subscribed this instrument; the Testator/Testatrix in their presence, subscribed the Will at the end and at the time of making the subscription declared the instrument to be the Testator/Testatrix's Last Will and Testament; at the request of the Testator/Testatrix and in the Testator/Testatrix's sight and presence and in the sight and presence of each other, all the subscribing witnesses witnessed the execution of the Will by the Testator/Testatrix by subscribing their names as witnesses to it; the Testator/Testatrix at the time of the execution of the Will, was over the age of 18 years and appeared to them of sound mind, memory and understanding and was in all respects competent to make a Will; and the Testator/Testatrix having declared to the said witnesses that he/she was not under any duress or any undue influence and that he/she voluntarily executed this will as his/her free act and deed.

      The subscribing witnesses further state that this affidavit was executed at the request of the Testator/Testatrix, and at the time of the execution of this affidavit the original Will, above described, was exhibited to them and they identified it as such Will by their signatures appearing on it as subscribing witnesses.

      The Testator/Testatrix states that each witness was and is competent and of a proper age to witness a will and further acknowledges that he/she has read the within instrument and he/she affirms that each and every statement made by the subscribing witness is true to his/her own knowledge.

Severally subscribed,        TESTATOR/TESTATRIX:  _____
acknowledged and sworn to
before me on _____      WITNESS:  _____

_____     WITNESS:  _____
Notary Public or Person
Authorized to Take Oaths          WITNESS:  _____

# Last Will and Testament

# of

_____

$\mathfrak{I}$, _____ , presently residing at

_____

being of full age and sound and disposing mind and memory, hereby make, publish and declare this to be my Last Will and Testament.

        FIRST: I hereby revoke any and all Wills and Codicils by me anytime heretofore made.

        SECOND: I direct all of my just debts and funeral expenses be paid out of my Estate as soon as practicable after my death.

        THIRD: I hereby nominate and appoint _____,
as Executor/Executrix of this, my Last Will and Testament, and I direct that no bond or other security shall be required of him/her in any jurisdiction. If my said Executor/Executrix hereinabove named is unable to serve as Executor/Executrix then I nominate and appoint _____,
Executor/Executrix of this my Last Will and Testament, and I further direct that he/she not be required to post any bond or other security.

        FOURTH: I hereby nominate and appoint _____
as Guardian of the person and property of my minor children. In the event that said Guardian hereinabove named shall be unable to serve as Guardian, then, and in such event I nominate and appoint
_____, Guardian/Co-guardians of the person and property of my minor child or children, and I direct that no bond shall be required of any Guardian herein.

        FIFTH: I give to my Executor/Executrix, authority to exercise all the powers, duties, rights and immunities conferred upon fiduciaries by law with full power to sell to mortgage and to lease, and to invest and reinvest all or any part of my Estate on such terms as he/she deems best.

        SIXTH:

_____

_____

_____

_____

IN WITNESS WHEREOF, I hereunto set my hand this _____ day of
_____, 19____ .

_____
(SIGN HERE)

Signed, sealed, published and declared by the above named Testator/Testatrix, as and for his/her Last Will and Testament, in the presence of us, who at his/her request, in his/her presence, and in the presence of one another have hereunto subscribed our names as attesting witnesses, the day and year last written above.

_____     residing at     _____
                                                    _____

_____     residing at     _____
                                                    _____

_____     residing at     _____
                                                    _____

Your Will is an important legal document. Have a qualified legal professional review it to verify that it is complete and faithful to your wishes, that it will direct your property where you want it to go, and that it will minimize the taxes on your estate. Laws can change; tell your attorney to contact you if laws change in such a way as to materially affect your Will.

# Instructions for #9 Will
# (Married Woman, Married Man, or Unmarried Person with Minor Children Making Specific Bequests)

Please have these instructions in front of you along with the #9 Will model. It is suggested that you complete the #9 Will using the #9 Will model as your general guide.

1. Your Will should be typed or printed in ink. Do not use a pencil or any other eraseable instrument.

2. Insert your full name, on the line below "LAST WILL AND TESTAMENT OF," and repeat your name and write your address on the next two lines.

3. In paragraph "THIRD," insert the name of the person that you want to serve as Executor/Executrix, and if that person does not survive you or is unable to serve for any reason, insert the name of an alternate Executor/Executrix.

4. In paragraph "FOURTH," insert the name of the person who you desire to be guardian of your minor child/children. In the event that this person does not survive you, or is unable to serve for any reason, insert the name of an alternate guardian.

5. In paragraph "SIXTH," write your specific bequests. Start your paragraph "SIXTH" with the following clause so that you won't forget "to give, devise and bequeath" your entire estate.

   "I hereby, give, devise, and bequeath my entire estate to _____, except for the following specific bequests." Insert the name of your chosen beneficiary on the blank line.

   At the end of paragraph "SIXTH," name an alternate beneficiary in the event that the above chosen beneficiary predeceases you. You may use the following clause:

   "If _____ shall die before me, then with the exception of the above bequests, I leave my entire estate to _____." Insert the name of your chosen beneficiary and alternate beneficiary on the blank lines.

6. Get your three witnesses together for the signing of the Will. In front of the three witnesses, date and sign the Will, at the same time telling the witnesses that this is your Last Will and Testament and that you want them to sign their names as witnesses to your Last Will and Testament. As soon as you are finished dating and signing the Will, have a witness sign his or her name and place his or her address on the line opposite his or her signature. *NOTE: It is important that no one leaves the room while each person is signing. In other words, each witness will witness your signature and the other witnesses' signatures.*

If you wish to self-prove your will, pull out the instructions for completing the Affidavit of Subscribing Witnesses.

Affidavit of Subscribing Witnesses

STATE OF _____)
                                                              ss.:
COUNTY OF _____)

On _____ , 19___ , personally appeared before me, the undersigned authority

1._____          2._____
           Testator/Testatrix                                      Witness

3. _____          4. _____
               Witness                                           Witness

known to me to be the Testator/Testatrix and Witnesses, respectively, who being severally sworn state under
oath that, all the subscribing witnesses witnessed the execution of the Will of the within named
Testator/Testatrix on the same date they subscribed this instrument; the Testator/Testatrix in their presence,
subscribed the Will at the end and at the time of making the subscription declared the instrument to be the
Testator/Testatrix's Last Will and Testament; at the request of the Testator/Testatrix and in the
Testator/Testatrix's sight and presence and in the sight and presence of each other, all the subscribing
witnesses witnessed the execution of the Will by the Testator/Testatrix by subscribing their names as
witnesses to it; the Testator/Testatrix at the time of the execution of the Will, was over the age of 18 years
and appeared to them of sound mind, memory and understanding and was in all respects competent to make
a Will; and the Testator/Testatrix having declared to the said witnesses that he/she was not under any duress
or any undue influence and that he/she voluntarily executed this will as his/her free act and deed.

              The subscribing witnesses further state that this affidavit was executed at the request of the
Testator/Testatrix, and at the time of the execution of this affidavit the original Will, above described, was
exhibited to them and they identified it as such Will by their signatures appearing on it as subscribing witnesses.

              The Testator/Testatrix states that each witness was and is competent and of a proper age to
witness a will and further acknowledges that he/she has read the within instrument and he/she affirms that
each and every statement made by the subscribing witness is true to his/her own knowledge.

Severally subscribed,                TESTATOR/TESTATRIX:    _____
acknowledged and sworn to
before me on _____          WITNESS:    _____

                                                        WITNESS:    _____

_____          WITNESS:    _____
Notary Public or Person
Authorized to Take Oaths

# Last Will and Testament

# of

_____

I,_____ , presently residing at

_____ ,

being of full age and sound and disposing mind and memory, hereby make, publish and declare this to be
my Last Will and Testament.

        FIRST: I hereby revoke any and all Wills and Codicils by me anytime heretofore made.

        SECOND: I direct all of my just debts and funeral expenses be paid out of my Estate as
soon as practicable after my death.

        THIRD: I hereby nominate and appoint _____ ,
as Executor/Executrix of this, my Last Will and Testament, and I direct that no bond or other security
shall be required of him/her in any jurisdiction. If my said Executor/Executrix hereinabove named is
unable to serve as Executor/Executrix then I nominate and appoint _____ ,
Executor/Executrix of this my Last Will and Testament, and I further direct that he/she not be required to
post any bond or other security.

        FOURTH: I give to my Executor/Executrix, authority to exercise all the powers, duties,
rights and immunities conferred upon fiduciaries by law with full power to sell to mortgage and to lease,
and to invest and re-invest all or any part of my Estate on such terms as he/she deems best.

        FIFTH:

_____

_____

_____

_____

_____

IN WITNESS WHEREOF, I hereunto set my hand this _____ day of
_____, 19____ .

_____
                                                                                        (SIGN HERE)

Signed, sealed, published and declared by the above named Testator/Testatrix, as and for his/her Last Will and Testament, in the presence of us, who at his/her request, in his/her presence, and in the presence of one another have hereunto subscribed our names as attesting witnesses, the day and year last written above.

_____        residing at        _____
                                                                                               _____

_____        residing at        _____
                                                                                               _____

_____        residing at        _____
                                                                                               _____

Your Will is an important legal document. Have a qualified legal professional review it to verify that it is complete and faithful to your wishes, that it will direct your property where you want it to go, and that it will minimize the taxes on your estate. Laws can change; tell your attorney to contact you if laws change in such a way as to materially affect your Will.

# Instructions for #10 Will
# (Married Woman, Married Man, or Unmarried Person Making Specific Bequests)

Please have these instructions in front of you along with the #10 Will model. It is suggested that you complete the #10 Will using the #10 Will model as your general guide.

1.　Your Will should be typed or printed in ink. Do not use a pencil or any other eraseable instrument.

2.　Insert your full name, on the line below "LAST WILL AND TESTAMENT OF," and repeat your name and write your address on the next two lines.

3.　In paragraph "THIRD," insert the name of the person that you want to serve as Executor/Executrix, and if that person does not survive you or is unable to serve for any reason, insert the name of an alternate Executor/Executrix.

4.　In paragraph "FIFTH," write your specific bequests. Start your paragraph "FIFTH" with the following clause so that you won't forget "to give, devise and bequeath" your entire estate.

　　"I hereby, give, devise, and bequeath my entire estate to ＿＿＿＿＿＿＿＿＿＿, except for the following specific bequests." Insert the name of your chosen beneficiary on the blank line.

　　At the end of paragraph "FIFTH," name an alternate beneficiary in the event that the above chosen beneficiary predeceases you. You may use the following clause.

　　"If ＿＿＿＿＿＿＿＿＿＿ shall die before me, then with the exception of the above bequests, I leave my entire estate to ＿＿＿＿＿＿＿＿＿＿." Insert the name of your chosen beneficiary, and alternate beneficiary on the blank lines.

5.　Get your three witnesses together for the signing of the Will. In front of the three witnesses, date and sign the Will, at the same time telling the witnesses that this is your Last Will and Testament and that you want them to sign their names as witnesses to your Last Will and Testament. As soon as you are finished dating and signing the Will, have a witness sign his or her name and place his or her address on the line opposite his or her signature. *NOTE: It is important that no one leaves the room while each person is signing. In other words, each witness will witness your signature and the other witnesses' signatures.*

　　If you wish to self-prove your will, pull out the instructions for completing the Affidavit of Subscribing Witnesses.

Affidavit of Subscribing Witnesses

STATE OF _____)

                                      ss.:

COUNTY OF _____)

On _____, 19___ , personally appeared before me, the undersigned authority

1. _____       2. _____
      Testator/Testatrix                             Witness

3. _____       4. _____
        Witness                                Witness

known to me to be the Testator/Testatrix and Witnesses, respectively, who being severally sworn state under oath that, all the subscribing witnesses witnessed the execution of the Will of the within named Testator/Testatrix on the same date they subscribed this instrument; the Testator/Testatrix in their presence, subscribed the Will at the end and at the time of making the subscription declared the instrument to be the Testator/Testatrix's Last Will and Testament; at the request of the Testator/Testatrix and in the Testator/Testatrix's sight and presence and in the sight and presence of each other, all the subscribing witnesses witnessed the execution of the Will by the Testator/Testatrix by subscribing their names as witnesses to it; the Testator/Testatrix at the time of the execution of the Will, was over the age of 18 years and appeared to them of sound mind, memory and understanding and was in all respects competent to make a Will; and the Testator/Testatrix having declared to the said witnesses that he/she was not under any duress or any undue influence and that he/she voluntarily executed this will as his/her free act and deed.

      The subscribing witnesses further state that this affidavit was executed at the request of the Testator/Testatrix, and at the time of the execution of this affidavit the original Will, above described, was exhibited to them and they identified it as such Will by their signatures appearing on it as subscribing witnesses.

      The Testator/Testatrix states that each witness was and is competent and of a proper age to witness a will and further acknowledges that he/she has read the within instrument and he/she affirms that each and every statement made by the subscribing witness is true to his/her own knowledge.

Severally subscribed,       TESTATOR/TESTATRIX:  _____
acknowledged and sworn to
before me on _____       WITNESS:  _____

                              WITNESS:  _____
_____
Notary Public or Person
Authorized to Take Oaths       WITNESS:  _____